The Cuban Revolution

About The Authors

Hugh S. Thomas—Lord Thomas of Swynnerton—an eminent historian and foreign policy adviser to British Prime Minister Thatcher, is currently Chairman of the Centre for Policy Studies, a leading British think tank. Educated at Cambridge University and at the Sorbonne, Lord Thomas served in the British Foreign Office and later became United Kingdom delegate to the United Nations. He also taught at the Royal Military Academy, Sandhurst, before becoming Professor of History and Chairman of Graduate Studies at the University of Reading, where he taught until 1976. Lord Thomas is the author of *Cuba: The Pursuit of Freedom*. He has also published *The History of the Spanish Civil War* (1961), *The Suez Crisis* (1967), and *The History of the World* (1979). Lord Thomas is the chairman of the CSIS Cuba Project working groups.

Dr. Georges Fauriol is a Fellow in Caribbean Basin Studies at the Georgetown University Center for Strategic and International Studies (CSIS). He is currently Director of the CSIS Cuba Project (the basis for this volume), the Immigration and National Security Project, as well as other Caribbean Basin efforts. He was previously associated with the Foreign Policy Research Institute and worked at the Inter-American Development Bank. Dr. Fauriol is the author of several publications: *Guatemala and Central America's Northern Flank, Caribbean Basin Security* (co-authored with Admiral Thomas Moorer), *The FAO, Immigration Policy and the National Interest, The Foreign Policy Behavior of Caribbean States,* "Caribbean Basin Environment: Policy Responses in the 1980s" in *Strategic Responses to Conflict in the 1980s,* and "The Americas" in *Strategic Requirements for the Army to the Year 2000.*

Juan Carlos Weiss is a Research Assistant in the Latin American Studies Program at CSIS. He has worked on Latin American foreign policy, security, and economic issues, particularly concerning Cuba, Mexico, and Brazil. He, along with William Perry, is the coauthor of "The Brazilian Defense Industry: Combining National Security With Commercial Success" (forthcoming 1984), "Lessons of the Cuban Revolution" (Washington Quarterly Winter Issue 1984) and co-editor and contributor to *Latin American Insurgency Movements* (forthcoming 1984). Mr. Weiss is the rapporteur for the CSIS Cuba Project.

About The Book

January 1984 marked the 25th anniversary of Fidel Castro's emergence to power. *The Cuban Revolution: 25 Years Later* is a product of the CSIS Cuba Project, a long-term effort to focus public as well as policymaker's attention on Cuba-related affairs. The lead author, Lord Thomas of Swynnerton, is the dean of political-historical studies on Cuba, and author of the encyclopedic *Cuba: The Pursuit of Freedom.*

A great deal of myth surrounds the evolution of Cuba since Castro's emergence to power over 25 years ago. Some of this myth is the product of official Cuban propaganda; some of it is also due to a generally misinformed American public. Sifting through available data to distinguish between fact and fiction, this book evaluates broadly the impact of Castro's regime on Cuba itself. Based on the findings of the CSIS Cuba Project, the book draws on the assessments of 18 top Cuban specialists on the political, economic, cultural, and social development of Cuba since 1959. In contrast to democracies such as Costa Rica, the equalization of society that has taken place under Castro's leadership has been accomplished by redistributing existing resources, not by creating new wealth. Moreover, the authors conclude that in politics, culture, and the economy, Cuba under Castro has become and remains rigid, stagnant, enormously militarized, and ideologically absolutist.

PUBLISHED IN COOPERATION WITH
THE CENTER FOR STRATEGIC AND INTERNATIONAL STUDIES
GEORGETOWN UNIVERSITY

CSIS Significant Issues Series
Volume VI, Number 11

Series Editors: Amos A. Jordan, William J. Taylor, Jr.
Editors: Jean C. Newsom, Nancy B. Eddy

The
Cuban Revolution
25 Years Later

Hugh S. Thomas
Georges A. Fauriol
Juan Carlos Weiss

Westview Press / Boulder and London

Published in 1984 in the United States of America by
    Westview Press, Inc.
    5500 Central Avenue
    Boulder, Colorado 80301
    Frederick A. Praeger, Publisher

Library of Congress Cataloging in Publication Data
Main entry under title:
The Cuban Revolution, 25 Years Later.
    (Significant issues series, ISSN 0736-7163; v. 6 no. 11)
    1. Cuba—History—1959–   2. Cuba—History—Revolution,
1959–Influence. I. Thomas, Hugh, 1931– II. Fauriol, Georges A. III. Weiss, Juan
Carlos. IV. CSIS Cuba Project. V. Series.
F1788.C827   1984   972.91′064   84-10315
ISBN 0-8133-7007-8

Composition for this book was provided by The Center for Strategic and International Studies.

Printed and bound in the United States of America
10   9   8   7   6

Contents

Foreword

The Center for Strategic and International Studies of Georgetown University is a policy center concerned with providing anticipatory, integrated assessments of major international issues confronting U.S. policymakers. The world about us is constantly changing, sometimes in ways that we only dimly perceive. This is a chronic problem in the Caribbean Basin where our attention is at best cyclical and rarely very thorough or insightful.

The Center's Latin American Studies Program is aimed at making a significant contribution to the development of a realistic, longterm strategy toward the area; a strategy that recognizes regional conditions, reflects U.S. interests, and is acceptable to the U.S. public. A central component of this contribution is the Cuba Project, which is an on-going effort to dispel some of the myths about Cuba and its revolution in order to establish a policy that is balanced and realistic.

This publication has been prepared by a working group involving a diverse mix of the most insightful analysts of Cuban affairs from this country and abroad. It makes a major contribution to an understanding of the domestic impact of Castro's revolution and his government.

Amos A. Jordan
President, CSIS

Introduction

E vents in the Caribbean Basin are at a critical juncture. Rising above the tide of rhetoric are dangerous trends for the region's political security and economic viability. At the epicenter of this geopolitical environment stands Cuba—foe to some, model to others.

The Castro revolution of 1959 now stands as a decisive landmark in the modern history of Latin America. Throughout Latin America the magnetism of Castro's personality, the indoctrination and regimentation of Cuban society, the communization of the economy, and the ruthlessness of the political system have aroused deep sentiments and caused striking developments within the region. Moreover, Cuba's impact over the last 25 years has acquired extra-hemispheric dimensions. In political and military affairs Havana has become a major influence in Third World radicalism and a key component of Soviet global strategy.

A reevaluation of the Castro regime is apropos on the occasion of the Cuban revolution's silver jubilee. In particular the question arises: what is the extent and significance of the thorough permutation of Cuba under Castro? In this period of reappraisals, the Cuban government remains eager to maintain and disseminate a self-created and assiduously cultivated image of constant positive achievements. The domestic transformation of Cuba's society has in fact been widely viewed as moving toward the development of a socialist environment. Although no longer viewed as a panacea for the problems of the developing world it is still widely proposed as a problem-solver for Latin America's social ills, if not those of the entire Third World. But to what degree are these much-publicized images myths? What are the significant feats of the Cuban regime since 1959?

Attention to these issues is essential to understanding one of the major challenges to the United States in the last quarter of the twentieth century. Ultimately, an assessment of Cuban dynamics is basic to an appreciation of the tasks this nation faces in Central America and elsewhere. Revolutionary overturns in the region as a whole have placed the Caribbean Basin at the very center of world politics. Thus, the comfortable historical circumstances that have allowed the American people largely to ignore and to deal ineffectually with the region, including Cuba, no longer exist.

Current foreign and domestic policy circumstances mandate an effort not only to highlight traditional concerns with Cuba, but also to reach and educate a wider public regarding Cuba's domestic condition in the 1980s. It is, after all, inconsistent for the United States to count human rights as a key issue in its Central American policy and ignore or neglect the systematic violations of human rights by the Castro regime. The CSIS Cuba Project thus constitutes the only full-scale effort, in and out of government, to address the Cuban revolution in all of its complex dimensions. Believing that an evaluation of Cuban international behavior first requires a baseline assessment of the nation's internal dynamics, the project has formed four Working Groups of distinguished experts to review the *domestic* sources of Cuban policy and conduct. It is this last aspect of the Cuban revolution that is the subject of this volume.

Under the chairmanship of Lord Thomas of Swynnerton, world-renowned Cuba scholar and presently foreign policy adviser to the British government, some 20 authorities on Cuban affairs addressed four broad aspects of Cuba's post-1959 society:

♦ *Political Control*
  Cuban communism
  the legal system
  the political elite
  the militarization of society
  rhetoric and reality in ideology
  bureaucratic management
  political succession

♦ *Economic Management*
  general economic trends
  efficiency and productivity
  economic diversification
  sectoral production
  foreign trade and external debt
  foreign assistance
  economic policy and ideology

♦ *Culture*
  Cuban culture and the arts
  popular culture and propaganda
  individual rights
  religion

♦ *Social Development of the Revolution*
health and human welfare
education
women in society
demographic trends
labor
rural/urban socialization

This review of Cuba's domestic revolution yields significant conclusions, including the following salient points:

1. The promised creation of a pluralistic society with elections and reforms of a social democratic nature based on the Cuban Constitution of 1940 never materialized;
2. Fidel Castro has radically and systematically transformed Cuba into a self-styled Marxist-Leninist dictatorship closely allied with and fully dependent on the Soviet Union for its short and long-term survival;
3. The argument that the U.S. somehow forced Castro to adopt Marxism-Leninism and align Cuba with the USSR is a historical fallacy;
4. The militarization of society appears to be the most striking accomplishment of the Cuban regime—the ideology has evolved into a mere justification of the militarization of society;
5. Fidel Castro's political priorities have remained fairly constant: maintaining undiluted power; making Cuba a world class actor on the basis of an extension of its own revolutionary activity; and institutionalizing a philosophy of anti-Americanism;
6. The lack of financial discipline, the erratic planning decisions, and the whimsical advocacy of unlikely products are prime causes for Cuba's relative economic failure since 1960. In effect the island has become the sugar cane plantation of the Soviet bloc;
7. Despite claims of extensive socioeconomic improvements, comparable and sometimes superior progress has occurred elsewhere in Latin America without the concomitant loss of political and economic freedoms;
8. As in other Communist states, the rights and interests of the individual have become subservient to the rights and interests of the state; laws and procedures encourage individual conformity, discourage individualism, and punish dissent. In effect, the Council of Ministers headed by Castro makes, interprets, and enforces the law;

9. The Cuban revolution cannot offer a single notable novelist, a famous poet, a penetrating essayist, not even a fresh contribution to Marxist analysis.

The world of ideas is often quite remote from the world of action. CSIS has kept this concern in mind in designing the project that has generated this report. The latter has benefitted from an extraordinary group of experts who participated in the deliberations of the Working Groups, out of which this report has evolved. These participants included:

Luis E. Aguilar, Georgetown University
Juan Benemelis, former Cuban official
Ernesto Betancourt, Economic consultant
Cole Blasier, University of Pittsburgh
Juan Clark, Miami Dade College
Sergio Díaz-Briquets, Demography consultant
Edward Gonzalez, RAND Corporation and UCLA
Paul Hollander, University of Massachusetts, Amherst
Irving Louis Horowitz, Rutgers University
Bruce McColm, Freedom House
Jorge Pérez-López, U.S. Department of Labor
William Ratliff, The Hoover Institution
Sergio Roca, Adelphi University
Jorge Sanguinetty, American University
Andrés Suarez, University of Florida
Lawrence Theriot, U.S. Department of Commerce

Background discussion papers for this project—some of which have appeared elsewhere and parts of which are included in this report—were prepared by Edward González (political control), Juan Clark (social development of the revolution), Luis Aguilar (culture), and Sergio Roca (economic management). Although this report drew substantially from these papers and particularly from the many discussions among the project participants, this is not, strictly speaking, a conference report. The authors alone assume responsibilty for the final product.

This report, although drafted by the three individuals whose names appear on the title page, also benefitted from additional critique by Miguel Sales, Kenneth Crosby, William Perry, Diego Abish, Lawrence Sternfield, Brian Lattel, Daniel Fitz-Simons, Adela María Bolet, and Armando Valladares. Likewise, without the devotion of the Cuba Project staff, the present effort would have been an unmanageable process. The assistance of Barbara Abbott and Lisa Frangos stands out. And finally, CSIS also acknowledges the support provided by the project donors, in particular The Cuban American National Foundation.

With the publication of this report, the Center's Cuba Project will be shifting its attention to Cuban international behavior. It is obvious that the U.S.-Cuban agenda is going to remain a delicate process for some time to come. For the sake of the national interest, further careful attention will clearly be required.

Georges Fauriol
Project Director
Senior Fellow
Caribbean Basin Studies

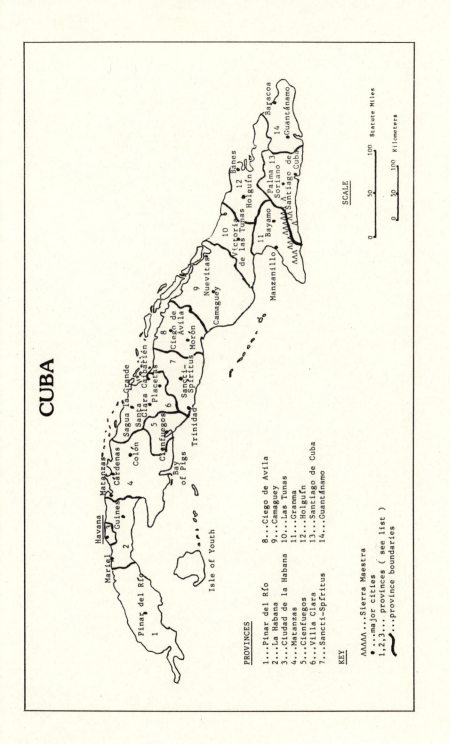

CUBA

PROVINCES

1...Pinar del Río
2...La Habana
3...Ciudad de la Habana
4...Matanzas
5...Cienfuegos
6...Villa Clara
7...Sancti-Spíritus

8...Ciego de Avila
9...Camaguey
10...Las Tunas
11...Granma
12...Holguín
13...Santiago de Cuba
14...Guantánamo

KEY

ΛΛΛΛ...Sierra Maestra
●...major cities
1,2,3...provinces (see list)
⌒⌒...province boundaries

SCALE

100 Statute Miles
0   50   100

0   50   100 Kilometers

1

Background

Since 1959 and under the leadership of Fidel Castro, Cuba has become the first Communist state in the Western Hemisphere. To the tragic surprise of many, who before 1959 had looked favorably upon Castro and the struggle against Cuban dictator Fulgencio Batista, the Cuban revolution changed direction abruptly soon after Batista fell. Promised social and democratic reform based on the Cuban Constitution of 1940 never materialized. Instead, Cuba was radically and systematically transformed into a self-styled Marxist-Leninist dictatorship, closely allied with and dependent upon the Soviet Union for survival—a model for the promotion of international revolutions.

Yet in the first few days of 1959, amid the confusion following the collapse of Batista's government, few could have predicted Cuba's ensuing transformation. Indeed, prior to Batista's fall there is little evidence that even the leaders of the various anti-Batista groups, including Fidel Castro, understood the precise nature of coming events.

Cuban Nationalism

The major motivating factors in the anti-Batista revolution were, undoubtedly, nationalism and the sense that only by violent means would Batista either reform his government or step down. Nationalism was a vibrant force in Cuba stemming back to the long period under Spanish colonialism. Cuba's greatest heroes, including many well remembered today—for example, José Martí—were all great nationalists who fought for independence from Spain. In the aftermath of the Spanish-American War, Cuba received its independence from Spain but then became in effect a dependency of the United States. Although the more onerous terms of U.S.-Cuban relations were discarded by Franklin D. Roosevelt, the United States has remained, by and large, the focus of Cuban nationalism during most of the twentieth century.

1

At one time relatively popular in Cuba, Batista lost much domestic and international support after he overthrew the democratically elected Cuban government in 1952. His corrupt practices cost him support, and his position was further eroded by underestimating the strength of his opposition while overestimating his own popular appeal. Thus in 1954, Batista committed a crucial error by granting general amnesty for political crimes. Fidel Castro was among those released. When Batista finally realized the threat to his government his responses were too little, too late, and generally self-defeating. Repressive measures drove great numbers into the opposition's camps and discredited the regime. This cycle ultimately led to Batista's collapse, but was resumed once again after Castro seized power and installed an even more efficient dictatorship.

The Influence of Communism

For the most part then, formal ideology played a minor role in motivating the "anti-Batistianos." There is little evidence that communism, for example, had a significant role in Batista's overthrow. Few of the many guerrilla groups, including Castro's 26 July Movement, were clearly ideologically oriented toward communism or supported by either the well-organized Cuban Communist party—known as the Popular Socialist Party (PSP)—or the Soviet Union.

Although in 1961 Castro claimed he had long been a Marxist-Leninist, on many occasions prior to 1961 he had made contrary claims. In fact, until 1958, he and the PSP were frequently at odds with each other. Castro condemned the PSP for selling out and participating in Batista's government. The PSP in turn opposed what they termed the "putschist" tactics and bourgeois objectives of the 26 July Movement. Furthermore the Soviet Union, backing the PSP, demonstrated no interest in Castro's group.

Castro: Perceptions and Deception

Castro and his followers were perceived in generally positive terms in the United States. As as result of highly favorable media coverage and his formidable public relations skills, Castro became something of a folk-hero in the United States and elsewhere. Although vague in specifics, the tone of Castro's proposed policies prior to 1959 gave no indication that traditionally close U.S.-Cuban relations would deteriorate under a Castro regime. Among his promises, Castro proposed early elections, diversification of Cuba's economy with U.S. assistance, and moderate social and political reforms based on the Cuban Constitution of 1940: opening up the political system, eliminating illiteracy, raising health and welfare standards, and curbing corruption and governmental repression. The only mention he made of nationalizing industry was to point out its impracticality. These promises allowed Castro to gather the support necessary to obtain power, which once obtained was quickly turned against many who had helped him achieve it.

Castro's enormous popularity rested on his charismatic role as the articulate guerrilla leader who, from his mountain headquarters, led the anti-Batista struggle. Yet Castro's strength was not as a military leader, but as a shrewd politician. He defeated Batista through political rather than military maneuvers—a public relations defeat. Batista was hurt more by the several well-publicized desertions of officers and enlisted men than by the few military engagements that actually took place. There were no major confrontations between the rebel forces and Batista's army in the period leading to the collapse of his government. Batista's army, in fact, was still largely intact, though demoralized, when he fled Cuba with most of his senior officers on New Year's Eve 1958.

1959: The Emerging Dictatorship

In January 1959, Castro quickly emerged as the most powerful and popular leader. Immediately thereafter the social-democratic nature of the movement began to erode while Castro's character became increasingly clear. In the first days of the Castro regime, his political power rested both in his substantial popularity and his control of the rebel army. Using both power bases Castro consolidated his position cautiously but systematically. Moderate members of the early "provisional" revolutionary government were totally powerless, and they either resigned in protest over the charade of authority or they were dismissed.

It did not take long for the extremist character of Castro's machinations to become clear. A ruthless but effective political opportunist with demonstrated ideological fluidity, Castro's primary passions were, and remain, unchallenged personal power, a sense of historical self-importance, and extreme Cuban nationalism.

Under Castro's guidance Cuban society was shaken violently, executions of political suspects became frequent, show trials of former government officials were televised, censorship was imposed, and dissent was crushed. The role of Cuban Communists in Castro's government increased greatly. Contacts were established with the

3

Soviet Union while threats and polemics were exchanged with the United States. The Bay of Pigs invasion afforded the Castro regime an opportunity to generate military and political capital. Castro was then able to eliminate much of the remaining opposition in Cuba and consolidate his ties with the USSR.

The record of Cuban-U.S. relations inevitably encouraged Castro to redress, at least partially, some of Cuba's many historical grievances against the United States. Anti-American nationalism, although a potent force in Cuba as elsewhere in Latin America, failed to provide a strong enough justification for his goals of unchallenged authority. Nor was it a powerful enough platform to achieve historical greatness. Castro therefore moved steadily toward the only ideology that could help him achieve his goals and the only country able to prop him up once he made that decision.

Marxism-Leninism and the USSR: A Formula for Dictatorship

In Marxism-Leninism and Soviet support, Castro found a formula that could satisfy his objectives as well as a justification for obliterating all U.S. influence in Cuba. Moreover, by turning to the Soviet Union Castro embraced the arch political, military, and philosophical rival of the United States, thus taking nationalist revenge in extreme terms. More important, the USSR was the only country capable of providing Castro and Cuba with the resources and support necessary to play a major role on the world stage.

The argument that the United States somehow forced Castro to adopt Marxism-Leninism and align Cuba with the USSR is a historical fallacy. Although it is likely that U.S. policy made the transition easier, there was nothing the United States or any other country could have done to prevent Castro from moving toward the Soviet Union. Given Castro's objectives of absolute power, a global role for Cuba, and a radical transformation of society, his options were limited.

The initial Soviet reaction to events in Cuba was decidedly cautious and unenthusiastic. By all accounts the Cuban revolution fit poorly into the Soviet strategy of fostering international communism through the cultivation of well established Communist parties, particularly those in Western Europe, while at the same time seeking peaceful coexistence with the West. The Soviet strategy in Europe had borne little fruit, however, and Soviet policy had begun to move toward the competing Chinese strategy of supporting Third World revolutions. The Chinese, for their part, though unable to provide

4

large-scale support, nevertheless enthusiastically embraced the Cuban cause. This recognition increased the likelihood that the Soviet Union, fearing a challenge to its role as the leading world Communist party, would be far more responsive to Castro's overtures seeking Soviet support.

The Crucial Years

The determining stage in Cuba's radical transformation ran from approximately January 1959 to 1962. During this period the full impact of the Cuban revolution occurred. (To refer to the Cuban revolution as still taking place in, say, 1970 is as inappropriate and incorrect as it is to refer to the Bolshevik revolution as still taking place in 1935.) The Cuban revolution began in earnest with Batista's flight from Cuba and ended soon after Castro's consolidation of power, his declaration of allegiance to Marxism-Leninism, and Cuba's full admission to the Soviet bloc. The tacit U.S. agreement not to invade Cuba, made after the 1962 Missile Crisis, virtually guaranteed the survival of Castro's regime. This allowed him to concentrate fully on strengthening his personal power, implementing radical domestic policies, and exporting revolution.

Although the fundamental nature of the regime was well established by the end of 1962, it continued to evolve after this time. Some changes have occurred in style, some in substance—few have been dramatic. A number of these transformations have reflected Cuban initiative, although others have been reactions to external pressures.

Since coming to power Castro's priorities remain unchanged: maintaining undiluted power; making Cuba a world class actor with major international influence; and, transforming Cuban society—in that order of priority. These themes must be kept in mind when considering the evolution of Cuba under Castro's rule.

2

Political Dimensions

Introduction

In the aftermath of the revolution that brought Fidel Castro to power in 1959, Cuba's political system was quickly transformed. Though the fundamental nature of Castro's regime was well established by about 1962, several features continued to evolve long after, the most notable involving changes in the structure and organization of Cuba's political system and foreign policies.

As these evolved, however, other characteristics remained relatively unchanged. Included among those are the nature of Castro's leadership, the role and makeup of Cuba's ruling elite, and the military's relationship to the rest of society. This section will focus both on those aspects that have evolved significantly and those that have remained static. Both sets of features will be assessed with a view toward their contemporary as well as their future implications for Cuba's political system.

Setting the Stage: Early Changes

Initial changes in Cuba's political system were rapid and largely in response to Castro's improvisations rather than to well-laid plans. As Castro consolidated his position further and the regime's survival became more secure, the pace of change slowed as the regime responded in a more measured manner to internal and external pressures.

Cuba in the 1960s was characterized not only by improvisation, but more important by radical sociopolitical and economic change and by the preeminence of Castro's charismatic leadership. The regime expanded its control of economic activities to an extent unprecedented in pre-1959 Cuba or elsewhere in Latin America. Newly created revolutionary organs—the militia, mass people's organizations, the Revolutionary Armed Forces (FAR), the Ministry of Interior (MININT), and eventually the new Cuban Communist

Party (PCC)—all penetrated society and mobilized it for defense, for economic purposes, or other tasks designated by the regime. One of the most radical changes that has occurred, however, is the total obliteration of Cuba's democratic infrastructure. To understand this transformation, one must begin with the Constitution of 1940.

The Destruction of Cuba's Democratic Infrastructure

In pre-Castro Cuba, the legal system was based essentially on the Constitution of 1940—considered by many as one of the most progressive in Latin America—as well as an Electoral Law and Penal Code that followed the French tradition prevalent throughout most of Latin America. These laws emphasized individual rights and clearly defined criminal and punishable actions. Protected by lifetime tenure, the judiciary was fairly independent.

From 1940 to 1952, despite irregularities in the use of power by the executive, the system functioned remarkably well. Although democratic Cuba had many problems, the violation of human rights was not one of them. Batista's 1952 military coup, however, changed the situation. Batista tried to minimize the impact of his illegal seizure of power by restoring normality, but the legitimacy of the regime was rejected by numerous sectors of Cuban society who insisted on a return to "true democracy." Soon, more radical opponents appeared. By 1957 Castro was fighting in the mountains, and the Revolutionary Student Federation had resorted to urban terrorism. The regime responded with increasing brutality, although the violations of human rights, illegal arrests, torture, and the killing of prisoners remained sporadic. Batista never organized the systematic elimination of the opposition nor did he impose total control over the press. Articles criticizing the regime were published and many political prisoners—most notably Fidel Castro and his followers— were allowed to go free in a general amnesty.

On December 31, 1958, Batista fled Cuba. The following day Castro entered Santiago de Cuba, announced the restoration of the 1940 constitution and proclaimed, to the surprise of many, "The revolution begins today!" The real meaning of that announcement unfolded rather rapidly. On January 13, the first five amendments, which radically modified the restored constitution, were enacted. One of them gave constitutional powers to the Council of Ministers. On February 7, the Council of Ministers repealed the Constitution of 1940 and replaced it with a Fundamental Law that considerably expanded the regime's capacity to override its own legal system. Article 38, for example, stated: "Every act which prohibits or limits

7

the participation of citizens in the political life of the nation is declared punishable." This shining democratic principle was rendered hollow by the addition of a transitory provision that declared: "Laws may be promulgated to limit or prohibit the participation in the political life of the nation by those individuals who, as the result of their public action and their participation in the electoral process under the tyranny, have aided the maintenance thereof." The provision marked the first break with Cuba's legal tradition, and the beginning of an authoritarian system characterized by its ambiguous definition of punishable actions. In this case, the vagueness of the term "public action" left almost all citizens at the mercy of the tribunals.

The Fundamental Law was a portent of things to come. The functions of the judiciary were partly taken over by "revolutionary tribunals," while the judges tenure of office was suspended by the Council of Ministers. A national purge followed. The majority of the members of the judiciary resigned, were forced out, or went into exile. Not even the revolutionary tribunals were free from official pressure.

The all-encompassing crime of "counterrevolutionary" hung over the entire population, and the tribunals were obliged to interpret the laws according to the political objectives of the regime. In August 1961, the Government Division of the Supreme Court proclaimed the "Socialist" character of the new Cuban revolutionary justice.

Like the judiciary, all other democratic institutions in Cuba crumbled under the regime's systematic pressure. Elections had been repeatedly promised during the anti-Batista struggle, but in June 1959, Fidel Castro launched a new slogan: "Revolution first, elections later!" The later was never determined. From then on, anyone who mentioned elections was considered a counterrevolutionary. Possibly to appease international criticism and maintain appearances, Castro did invent a new political formula, direct democracy. The approving roars of a multitude gathered in a plaza became the source of legitimacy, the true voice of the people. The presence of half a million Cubans at the People's Second Assembly, held in Havana on February 14, 1962, proved that Cuba was, according to Castro, "the most democratic government in the Americas." Curiously, many outsiders have been impressed by the argument without considering the dangers of dissent against a mob. Whether it is sound to assume that in a nation of 10 million the applause of 500 thousand could represent the true feelings of the entire population remains an open question.

8

With direct democracy officially proclaimed, there were no independent newspapers in Cuba; all television and radio stations were expropriated. Political groups and parties, including the 26 July Movement were forced to join the Integrated Revolutionary Organizations (ORI), from which the new Cuban Communist Party would eventually emerge. Labor unions were compelled to accept leaders selected by the regime and all Catholic and private schools were closed. On July 26, 1965 Castro proclaimed: "In Cuba when we say party we mean government, and when we say government we mean party." Castro's repressive measures combined with the Socialist Constitution of 1975, restructured the Cuban legal order and eliminated all traces of Western democracy.

Changing Features

By the start of the 1970s, the Cuban political system was embarking on a complete structural reorganization. Improvisation, radical change, and the charismatic basis of the regime, gave way to a more regimented, regularized, and predictable political order closely modeled after the Soviet Union. The Cuban Communist Party was expanded and given greater prominence. A more rational administrative apparatus was introduced, as well as new state and government organs. Moreover, greater attention was focused on upgrading the army and narrowing its role to solely military tasks.

The Cuban Communist Party

The development of the PCC was accelerated so that it could assume a position in Cuba parallel to that of the Communist party in the Soviet Union. In contrast to the Bolsheviks, however, the old Cuban Communist party (PSP) had played a negligible role in the Cuban revolution and consequently occupied a secondary role in Cuba's regime throughout most of the 1960s. Even after a new Cuban Communist party was established in 1965, the party remained firmly in Castro's control and was not an independent institution in the Soviet sense.

Throughout the 1960s there was virtually no distinction between the PCC and the Cuban government. Although the PCC was structured around outlines similar to the Soviet Communist Party—with a Central Committee, a Political Bureau, and a General Secretariat— its small membership met infrequently and did not have an independent leadership or policymaking role. In the early 1970s the PCC expanded its membership beyond its predominantly military core and received conspicuously greater political prominence. This

9

change peaked in 1975 with the first PCC Party Congress in which a new Cuban constitution was put forward and Fidel and Raúl Castro were voted First and Second Secretary, respectively, of the General Secretariat.

The Government Infrastructure

In 1972 the principal administrative organ of the government, the Council of Ministers, was reorganized and an Executive Committee was created to act in an overall supervisory role. In addition to the post of chairman—held by the prime minister—a number of deputy prime ministers were established in a fashion similar to Soviet posts, with each deputy prime minister responsible for managing a combination of state agencies, ministries, and institutes. Later, the Executive Committee was again reorganized with Fidel Castro as president, Raúl Castro as first vice president, and several new vice presidential positions.

New institutions were developed to provide the masses with a vehicle for more meaningful political participation at the grass roots level. Such participation augmented the leadership's traditional practice of mobilizing the masses to implement the revolutionary tasks ordained from above. As a consequence, participatory vehicles were first introduced with trade union elections in 1973. They became still more prevalent with the convening of national elections for the National Assembly of People's Power and the implementation of the "Poder Popular" (which became island-wide in 1976). In the former, rank-and-file trade union members were consulted on changes in labor policy, while in the latter residents were given new opportunities to participate in the administration of their local communities. With the Second Party Congress in 1980, the inclusion of new members in the expanded Central Committee seems to suggest an objective designed to incorporate intermediate elites at higher levels of both party and government, thereby broadening the elite basis of the regime.

Professionalization of the Military

The regularization of political processes also affected the Cuban military. From the earliest days of the revolution, the military had been the most powerful Cuban institution—the Castro base of personal power—and was often involved in the civilian sector. Originally little more than a poorly trained and equipped guerrilla army numbering no more than a few hundred men, the regular army grew to over 225 thousand highly-trained, well-equipped soldiers. Though

10

ranking eighth in Latin America in population, Cuba's military establishment is only slightly smaller than Brazil's, whose population is over 10 times larger. The Cuban armed forces are arguably the most powerful, and certainly the most experienced in the hemisphere, aside from the United States.

Since 1959, Castro has controlled FAR as commander-in-chief and commanded the troops through the ministry of the interior, and has retained the right to create or disband militias at will. With few exceptions, nearly the entire Cuban leadership came from the military's ranks. To date, the highest leadership in contemporary Cuba remains military or formerly military personnel whose careers began as followers of Fidel or Raúl Castro in the pre-1959 guerrilla army.

Throughout the 1960s the military as an institution was often directly involved in civilian affairs, including many production tasks, usually because it was the only institution possessing sufficient technical and managerial expertise and organized manpower. Toward the late 1960s and early 1970s, however, the military focused greater attention on upgrading its level of professionalism and specialization while turning many non-military tasks back over to the civilian sector. Militias and paramilitary youth brigades were disbanded or reorganized and integrated into the Cuban armed forces. Subsequently, FAR was slowly reorganized along Soviet lines while receiving increasingly sophisticated arms and training.

Although the specifics of Soviet influence are unclear, this influence in Cuban affairs is substantial—particularly within the military structure. In addition to the nature and organization of the Cuban military, which is based on the Soviet model, and the presence of Soviet troops in Cuba, the two institutions are intricately linked at the operational level. In fact, coordination between the two militaries—as well as the linkage of intelligence services—predates coordination between the party and the bureaucracy. In the 1970s these links were reinforced by heightened cooperation between Cuba and the Soviet Union in expanded Cuban international military activities.

Foreign Policies

In contrast to the 1960s, during which time Castro maintained a policy of sending small bands of guerrillas to foment revolutionary upheaval throughout Latin America, in the 1970s Castro's scope of international activities extended throughout Africa and the Middle East as well as into Latin America and included large-scale mobilization of regular troops as well as guerrilla activity. In the second half of the 1970s, Cuba dispatched 36 thousand combat troops to

11

Angola and an additional 12 thousand troops to Ethiopia. These two expeditionary forces were critical to the military victories and consolidation of power achieved by the Marxist regimes in both African countries.

Cuban forces abroad in the late 1970s accounted for two-thirds of the military and technical personnel stationed by all Communist states in the Third World—exceeding Soviet troops in Afghanistan and Vietnamese forces in Southeast Asia. In addition to troops, Cuba dispatched technicians, advisers, and construction workers to Algeria, Iraq, Jamaica, Libya, Mozambique, Nicaragua, Vietnam, and Grenada in the late 1970s and early 1980s.

At the time of its African activities, Cuba also began pursuing an activist policy in the Caribbean Basin. Beginning in 1977, Havana increased its backing for the Sandinistas in their battle against the Somoza government in Nicaragua. Indeed, the large infusion of Cuban war material in spring 1979 was the key to the Sandinista National Liberation Front's (FSLN) final offensive that ultimately toppled the Somoza regime. Cuba's capable, behind-the-scenes management of revolutionary tactics paved the way for a broad political coalition in which the Sandinistas were to hold the key to power. Cuba then mounted major civilian and military technical assistance programs to Nicaragua, where by 1983 some 6,000 Cuban civilian personnel were assisting the Nicaraguan government in the fields of public health, education and administration. Another 2,000 advisers and trainers from FAR and MININT were rapidly building Nicaragua's military and internal security capabilities in connection with the Soviet Union, East Germany, and other Eastern bloc countries.

In sum, both the scope and form of Cuban international involvement has been truly remarkable for an island-state with a population of only 10 million and a semi-developed economy that can barely satisfy the basic needs of its citizens. In terms of magnitude, over 100 thousand regular and ready-reserve personnel in the Cuban armed forces, according to Castro, had served in the African campaigns by the end of 1980. Cuba had some 70 thousand military troops and advisers, along with civilian technicians and advisers, in 23 countries worldwide in 1982. Closer to home, Cuba's political and manpower investments in Central America were extensive, and despite the loss of Grenada in 1983, Cuban influence in the Caribbean remains significant. More tragically, Cuba's internationalism has also demonstrated Havana's readiness not only to sacrifice domestic economic needs for the sake of foreign policy priorities, but also a great readiness to shed Cuban blood in far-off battlefields.

Although Cuba's record of foreign activities is extensive and well known, its motives and the extent of its successes and failures are the subject of much debate. There are, however, two basic arguments for Cuba's decision to send troops overseas in the 1970s. The first holds that following the improvisational nature of Cuban politics during the 1960s and the dismal failure of the Cuban economy—particularly after the disastrous 1970 harvest—the Soviet Union sought to introduce a greater degree of institutionalization into the Cuban political system. By their very nature, such changes would have resulted in a dimunition of Castro's power, something Castro has been unwilling to accept. The argument continues that following the successful performance of 500 Cuban tank commanders fighting for Syria in the Yom Kippur War in 1973, Castro decided to offer an active militarized foreign policy attractive to the Soviet Union as a quid pro quo for continued strong Soviet commitment.

A second line of reasoning suggests that Castro has had ambitions all along to occupy an active international leadership position. Following his failure to strengthen Cuba's economy during the 1960s, Castro accelerated the pursuit of his foreign policy ambitions so that he achieved the success abroad that he was not able to attain domestically. Regardless of his motives (which in all likelihood are a combination of both arguments: internal and external pressures and personal ambition) the scope of Cuban international activities is astounding for a country of Cuba's size and limited resources and could not be achieved without large-scale economic and military support from the Soviet Union.

Constant Features

Notwithstanding many symbolic and some substantive changes that occurred during the evolution of the Cuban political system under 25 years of Fidel Castro's rule, several features of the nature of the regime have remained relatively constant. First, despite efforts to create a more institutionalized system, Castro remains the overarching figure within Cuban politics. Second, under the institutionalization of the political process, the power of the small elite, consisting almost exclusively of close pre-1959 followers of Fidel and Raúl Castro, has been formalized and greatly enhanced. Moreover, the Cuban political process continues to provide a framework in which this revolutionary elite is able to monopolize political power, achieve radical societal change, and promote economic development. And third, characteristic of the Cuban regime is the continued militarization of the Cuban political system.

Although Castro's level of popularity has varied with his successes and failures, since coming to power in 1959 he has remained the overwhelming political force in Cuba. Castro's personalist and charismatic rule, not unlike Mao's rule in China and Tito's in Yugoslavia, is the central feature of Cuban politics.

The extent of his personal power is unsurpassed. Castro is first secretary of the Communist party and commander-in-chief of the armed forces, as well as president of both the Council of State and the Council of Ministers. In sum, he holds the top leadership post in the party, state, government, and armed forces; a Cuban phenomenon unmatched elsewhere either in the Soviet Union or among its East European allies.

In analyzing Castro's rule, it is evident that his primary motive and objective has always been to maintain the undiluted power needed to carry out his destined historical role as a great revolutionary torchbearer. Everything else is of a lower priority, and he has opposed any activity, law, or reform—including economic reform—that involves a diminution of his political power. Over time, Fidel Castro, as a political opportunist, has changed and adapted to circumstances whenever necessary to preserve his power and enable him to pursue his unchanging primary goals.

Since 1961 Castro has labeled himself as a Marxist-Leninist and proclaimed the Cuban revolution a communist revolution. Yet it has never been quite clear whether Castro's affinity for Marxism-Leninism is sincere or is simply a label of convenience. Whether Fidel Castro was a believing Communist prior to 1959 is uncertain at best. Moreover, unlike revolutionary or post-revolutionary leaders in China or the Soviet Union who claimed great affinity for Marxist theory and principles or, in any case, frequently used it to justify what they did, Castro seldom refers to Marxism-Leninism and has contributed little to it.

Indeed, his leadership style is characterized by a combination of romantic, anti-American, "anti-imperialist," and authoritarian populism that is rooted more in personal ambition and Cuban nationalism than in abstract ideology.

Castro's contribution to political leadership has come in his development of a relatively unique combination of political-military leadership that is characterized by the militarization of politics, rather than the other way around, and it is in this style that the ongoing power and influence of the narrow ex-guerrilla elite is most evident.

The Revolutionary Elite

Throughout the history of the Cuban revolution, a core elite consisting of the pre-1959 civilian and military followers of Fidel and Raúl Castro has, to varying degrees, been preeminent within the political system. In recent years, Cuba has witnessed the narrowing of this elite and its renewed concentration of power to an extent unprecedented since the 1960s. The most peculiar aspect of Cuba's limited ruling group is in fact its familiar dimension. Concurrently, as Fidel occupies the top offices in the party, state, government, and armed forces, Raúl occupies the second highest office in each: Raúl Castro is the second secretary of the party, first vice president of both the Council of State and Council of Ministers; he is the minister of defense, as well as the highest ranking military officer.

The role of Fidel and Raúl Castro's followers can be seen in the composition of the Communist party's leading organs as announced at the Second Party Congress in December 1980. In the newly enlarged Political Bureau, only 3 out of its 16 members do not trace their careers back as early guerrilla followers of Fidel or Raúl Castro.

Notwithstanding the inclusion of lower and middle level elites in the 225 member Communist Party Central Committee, Fidel and his brother, together with their closest associates, continue to monopolize the most important organs of policy-making and power in the party, the armed forces, internal security organs, and in the state and government councils and ministries. The power and preeminence of this small group is related to another distinct feature of the Cuban political system—the predominant role played by the military both at the elite and mass levels. As already noted, a core group of ex-revolutionaries—all guerrilla veterans—hold many of the top civilian and military leadership positions. Moreover, in contrast to traditional authoritarian regimes in Latin America, Cuba's political order has based itself from the very start on both the organization and mobilization of mass support. Thus, in addition to armed forces that number a quarter million men in uniform, the military impact on society is evident in such organizations as the paramilitary Territorial Troop Militia, numbering 1 million members, and the non-military but regimentalized 5.3 million member Committees for the Defense of the Revolution.

The Militarization or Regimentation of the Political System

The Revolutionary Armed Forces, antedating all other revolutionary sectors of the Cuban political system including the Communist party, has traditionally absorbed the best talent in the country and has become a feeder institution providing much of the civilian sector's leadership. The Cuban military is clearly professionalized in the sense that it is well-trained, educated, equipped, and disciplined—particularly in relative terms to other Latin American armed forces. On the other hand, the military's participation in civilian affairs is unprecedented not only in Latin America but also in other countries with ruling Communist parties—except in times of martial law. Moreover, the seamlessness between the military and the civilian sectors is compounded by the fact that one family controls both the army and the political structure.

Although it is clear that the Revolutionary Armed Forces have long been the foundation upon which Castro's personal power is based, he has often felt it necessary to check FAR's power. Indeed, Castro has several times used his authority to create new domestic military organizations, outside the jurisdiction of the armed forces, as a sort of counterweight to the growing influence of the latter. Yet, at the same time, it has been through the armed forces that Castro has achieved his only major political successes. This fact has both enhanced the preeminence of the military over the civilian sector— which has experienced many failures—and strengthened Castro's personal power.

Analyzing the Cuban System

Institutionalization or Bureaucratic Trappings?—A Debate

One of the major debates among analysts of Cuban politics has been the question of the so-called "institutionalization" of the Cuban political system. This came about as an attempt to define the changes that occurred in Cuba between the 1960s and the 1970s. Despite a reorganization of the political system, it has been argued that the institutionalization of the Castro regime, if this has occurred at all, has occurred only in the broadest sense of the word. In a narrow sense, institutionalization implies the subordination of individuals to institutions—that is, the latter having power and preeminence over the former throughout the political process. In Cuba, this has not taken place, particularly as the top leadership levels remain above the law.

On the other hand, if one defines institutionalization broadly, since the mid-1970s an attempt has been made to create a more ordered political process and precise definition of the relationship between the state, its organs, and the individual. This is exemplified by the creation of a new Council of State, and a National Assembly of People's Power, which resembles that of the Presidium and Supreme Soviet in the USSR, while the Council of Ministers and other governmental administrative organs are differentiated from these new bodies. The PCC was strengthened and greatly expanded to over 434 thousand regular and candidate members by 1980, and its proceedings regularized. As with the Soviet Communist Party, the revitalized PCC is to lead and monitor society and government rather than engage in administration; this clearly differentiates party functions and responsibilities from those of government.

On the other hand, it is doubtful that this formalization of political processes has, in any substantial manner, altered the nature of the regime. The indigenous factors in Cuban politics—specifically, the powerful personality of Fidel Castro—could not be subsumed by the new emphasis given to creating viable political institutions. On the contrary, in the end institutionalization has formally recognized the newly redistributed and reconcentrated political power held by Fidel and his brother, along with their civilian and military followers from the Moncada and Sierra Maestra struggles.

The motives for the introduction of greater bureaucratic formality, and the reasons for its limited impact, are two-fold. On the one hand, in response to internal as well as external pressures the regime was encouraged to adjust its political processes. Given the substantial Soviet role in Cuba, the adjustment took the form of a structural reorganization of political and administrative organs around Soviet lines. Yet the basic nature of Castro's rule has made it unlikely that he would give up any degree of significant power.

By the start of the 1980s, therefore, institutionalization appears to have done little to diminish the personalistic character of Cuban politics, at least at its highest levels. Although a more ordered and standardized political process is now in existence, Fidel Castro and the elite of guerrilla veterans remain central to that process. The structural reorganization of Cuba's political system has had a somewhat formalizing effect at the middle levels of power, but it has also had an enshrining impact at the highest levels of political authority.

A Political Model For Cuba: The Garrison State

It is useful to try to develop frameworks of analysis in order to evaluate the evolution of Cuba's political system, and perhaps even its future trajectory. Considerable attention may be given to a portrait that some have argued most accurately describes Cuba's political system—the garrison state model as developed by the Argentine

17

political scientist Guillermo O'Donnell. Its principal features include the militarization of society; the government monopolization of public opinion and all social, economic, and political activity; mass radicalization; and the idea of constant warfare against both internal and external enemies. It need not mean that the military runs the state, but it does suggest that "experts of violence" are in power.

Several of these characteristics clearly apply to Cuba in the 1980s. The top leadership throughout the state, government, and party apparatus are with few exceptions all military or former military personnel. Moreover, the militarization of society has increased steadily and has become part of the political culture, beginning with early education. By constantly mobilizing the population for internal war, the elite is able to achieve its top two priorities: that of preserving their powerful positions and of maintaining their ability to wage revolutionary wars on an international scale.

Historically, there is in Cuba's evolution much to lend credibility to this analysis. The roots of the garrison state can be found in the predominance given by Castro to the military, which has long served as a feeder institution supplying leadership for civilian posts. In the late 1960s the military was increasingly relied upon for internal domestic purposes—sometimes to augment civilian institutions, often to carry out the tasks that civilian institutions were incapable of fulfilling. Since the early 1970s, however, the military has increasingly confined itself to military matters, concentrating on strengthening its capabilities to launch into international ventures.

In a parallel development, there was a period of change in the civilian sector, including the creation of new organizations and the introduction of more efficient methods of operation. Although the military was largely successful in its efforts, the civilian domestic sector was not. The military was the lead agent for transforming Cuba into a world class actor, raising its international status and increasing Cuba's leverage with the Soviet Union. As a result, the late 1970s witnessed the reemergence of the power and preeminence of the elite core of guerrilla veterans, along with the military as an institution.

Cuba in Contrast to Other Communist States

Despite the attractiveness of the garrison state model in its usefulness for evaluating Cuba, it is clear that the country's political evolution after a quarter of a century of Castro's rule is difficult to place in a neat political mold. Although Cuba shares important characteristics with other Communist states its political development has differed from most of them.

First, the Cuban revolution was not led by a Communist party nor an openly Marxist leadership. As a result, the core of the regime comes not from the pre-1959 Communist party but from leaders of the 26 July Movement. Second, Cuba has been the only Communist state established within the traditional U.S. sphere of influence. But because of the uniqueness of Cuba's proximity to the United States, the cult of anti-American sentiment generated by the Castro regime is probably much stronger than in other socialist countries, and sometimes surpasses Marxism-Leninism as a force in mobilizing mass support for the regime. Finally, Cuba's ultimate economic and political dependence upon the Soviet Union greatly exceeds that of any other socialist state. The attempt to marry Cuban society and its Latin cultural traditions, with a Russian version of communism, however, has sometimes produced contradictory results. Cuba's political institutions and infrastructure are modeled after the Soviet Union, yet Cuba's political system is uniquely Cuban. For example, the role of Castro, the pre-1959 guerilla elite, and the military are unlike anything in the Soviet Union or Eastern Europe. On the other hand, many of Cuba's socioeconomic reforms resemble Soviet models and could not have occurred without massive Soviet largesse. Ironically, Cuban economic dependence on the Soviet Union is far greater than it ever was on the United States.

Conclusions

Although the Castro regime has certainly evolved in several aspects since coming to power in the early 1960s, its essential character has remained virtually unchanged. On the one hand, it is evident that there has been a clear effort to reorganize some existing state structures and processes and to create some new ones. Thus, the PCC was expanded both in size and functions, the government and state apparatus was reorganized, and the armed forces were upgraded and professionalized. In foreign policy, Cuba has developed its role from supporting small guerrilla "foco" groups in rural Latin America in the 1960s to mounting large-scale troop deployments in Africa in the 1970s.

Notwithstanding these and other changes, however, Castro's personal leadership, with its emphasis on highly centralized authority and ambitious foreign policy objectives, remains the dominant feature in Cuban politics, as does the influence of the small veteran ex-guerrilla elite. Moreover, Cuban society continues to be organized as one giant military state. The evolution of the Cuban political system since 1959 has, in effect, modified some structural features while leaving unchanged the basic character of the Castro dictatorship.

3

Economic Dimensions

Introduction

In 1959 the appeal of Fidel Castro and the still nascent Cuban revolution lay, in large part, in promises and expectations of a brighter economic future for Cuba. Yet, after more than a quarter of a century under Castro and communism the Cuban economy has, on balance, fared poorly. Given the secretive nature of Cuba's political system and its frequently unorthodox economic management techniques, precise economic data is difficult to obtain, and as a result, efforts to conduct comprehensive studies are often hindered. Sufficient information is available, however, to produce sound, although broad, evaluations of Cuba's economic performance.

In general, Cuba's economy under Castro has suffered from several major weaknesses. Structural imbalances have led to the overspecialization of production together with an overreliance on a single trading partner. Moreover, despite—or perhaps partially because of—large-scale Soviet aid and assistance, Cuba's economic growth has been erratic and often weak. Indeed, Cuba's long-term economic performance under Castro pales in contrast to the long-term performance of most Latin American nations.

In addition to a brief evaluation of Cuba's economy in structural features, growth pattern, and international comparisons, this chapter will explore the impact of ideology, political priorities, military policies, and the U.S. embargo on the Cuban economy.

Structural Imbalances

Despite promises to the contrary, the Castro regime has been unable to correct many of the structural flaws of the pre-revolutionary economy, and in several respects the Cuban economy is now weaker than it was prior to Castro's rule. Pre-revolutionary Cuba was characterized both by a concentration on sugar production as the nation's principal economic activity and a trade dependency

20

with one partner—the United States. Other features included widespread unemployment and marked differences in urban-rural living standards. Although the Castro regime has at times made efforts to address these structural imbalances, the results have been generally poor. Indeed, after 25 years both sugar dependency and trade concentration remain essentially unaltered and, in fact, have increased somewhat, although the Community for Mutual Economic Assistance (COMECON) has replaced the United States as Cuba's main trading partner. And despite the fact that open unemployment is low, disguised unemployment in the form of low labor productivity is substantial. Moreover, urban-rural inequalities still persist, although there have been some significant accomplishments, notably in the rural education and health sectors. Finally, growing inflation, trade deficits, and external debts are features of Castro's Cuba.

The production and export of sugar has remained Cuba's economic mainstay. In spite of early efforts to diversify the economy, sugar has represented over 80 percent of the total value of Cuban exports since 1959 and as recently as 1982 it accounted for 83 percent. Under Castro's rule, sugar has increased as a percentage of total agricultural output as well as total economic output. At the same time, industry has declined over 12 percent as a share of total economic output. Because world sugar prices are subject to extreme fluctuations, Cuba must rely on high Soviet subsidies to maintain some measure of economic stability. World sugar prices, for example, fell 75 percent from 1980 to 1982. Consequently, the value of Cuba's 1982 sugar output—the second largest in its history—was below that of the much smaller 1980 harvest. In fact, the 1982 price of seven cents per pound was probably below production costs. The Soviet Union, together with the rest of the Eastern bloc, purchases over 60 percent of Cuba's sugar, paying Cuba four times the world price.In fact, the Eastern bloc purchases a larger percentage of Cuba's sugar output than did the United States prior to 1959.

Cuba's failure to diversify its sugar based economy is the result of political as well as economic decisions on Castro's part. To a large degree, Cuba's sugar specialization remains a function of comparative advantage. Given Cuba's natural resources, extensive industrial and agricultural diversification would involve careful and realistic planning, access to major markets for trade, large-scale capital investment, and most importantly, commitment to economic development objectives over political goals. Although Cuba attempted to diversify in the early 1960s, it failed totally because of unrealistic and poorly planned strategies.

Cuba's specialization in sugar production requires that it maintain an open economy—that is, it must trade to obtain those goods it does not produce. This requires a close relationship with a large and powerful trading partner. There are only three major world sugar markets: the United States, Western Europe, and the Eastern bloc. Once Cuba became politically aligned with the Soviet Union it lost all access to its natural major trading partner and market—the United States. It could also no longer participate in many regional trade arrangements in this hemisphere, and for various reasons it has no access to Western European markets. Consequently, the Soviet Union and its client states offered the only major market. Within the Eastern bloc's trade organization, COMECON, however, Cuba was the best suited to produce sugar. It was the only product Cuba could produce in quantity at a natural comparative advantage. In effect, Cuba was assigned the role of the Eastern bloc's sugar plantation.

The designation of Cuba as the sugar supplier for the Communist world does not, however, preclude the possibility nor the desirability of some modicum of diversification. In Cuba there has always been a wish to diversify the economy, particularly to achieve agricultural self-sufficiency. To this end, diversification has been attempted in many different areas, but it has almost always failed because these attempts have been characterized by a high degree of improvisation along with unrealistic goals. In many cases, however, efforts at diversification were merely an attempt to showcase Communist Cuba's economic potential and viability. An example here would be the attempt to establish large-scale pork and beef cattle industries.

In addition to the failure to diversify Cuba's economy, Castro has failed to alter the nation's traditional dependence on one market. All told, over 86 percent of Cuba's trade is with Communist states. Moreover, this dependency is likely to increase. In the summer of 1981 Cuba signed long-term agreements with several Eastern bloc countries committing it to significant increases in sugar deliveries through 1990—increases it may not be able to achieve without deleterious side-effects elsewhere in the economy.

Cuba has also been unable to overcome many problems characteristic of a capitalist as well as a socialist economy. The island suffers from debilitating bottlenecks, low labor productivity, inefficiency, and absenteeism characteristic of socialist economies. In addition, Cuba has been unable to eradicate productivity and unemployment problems.

Unemployment was initially reduced by converting unemployment into underemployment; the economy did not expand, rather, more people were hired. It was also reduced as greater numbers of youths remained in school longer and because the number of exiles grew. In addition, a bloated bureaucracy, a vastly enlarged military and the export of troops and workers absorbed some of the unemployment. Despite these measures unemployment still exists, and productivity and efficiency have declined.

Since 1979, Cuba's leadership has acknowledged the existence of open unemployment in several economic sectors for a total of some 5 to 6 percent of the entire labor force. In all likelihood unemployment will continue to grow as population growth exceeds economic growth. Cuban leaders have also openly recognized widespread problems with underemployment or disguised unemployment—full-time work with low productivity or severe overstaffing—and general inefficiency. In 1981, heavy construction equipment was unused 61 percent of scheduled time. In a similar period, 68 percent of industrial investment projects were not completed on schedule.

Although Castro's regime has failed to eliminate, or even reduce, several basic structural flaws, it can be credited with some notable achievements. The most impressive revolutionary accomplishment has been the reduction of pre-revolutionary inequalities in urban-rural living standards and, to a certain extent, in income distribution. But assessments of these changes are difficult because of unavailable data. They must therefore be made with caution. In general, more educational and health services are available to the rural population; nevertheless, significant gaps remain. There is, for example, a 20 percent difference in average urban-rural illiteracy rates and a large gap in wages. The top 10 percent of wage earners—usually urban—receive wages up to 10 times higher than the bottom 10 percent who are, invariably rural agricultural laborers. Moreover, the quality of certain social services available to some segments, including what was once the urban middle class, may have deteriorated compared to past standards. Overall, the distribution of social services is more balanced than before 1959, though far from equitable. In 1959 the ratio of physicians to population ranged from 1 to 263 in urban areas to 1 to 1,750 in rural areas. And although in recent years some 60 percent of new hospital beds have been assigned to rural provinces, the total rural bed population ratio of 1.7 to 1,000 still lags far behind Havana's 9.9 to 1,000 rate. Furthermore, rural areas have fared poorly in terms of new housing and the distribution of consumer durables in which urban centers retain clear advantages.

For the most part, Cuba like many other Communist countries, has been unable to improve its poor performance in the distribution of consumer goods and delivering public services efficiently. In addition to persistent housing problems, the government continues to be plagued with troublesome performance in the provision of local transportation, consumer goods and services, medical care, restaurants, water supply, sewer systems, electric service, and other basic services. As an example, in the late 1970s, there was an estimated housing deficit of 700 thousand units—housing construction has never exceeded 21 thousand annually.

Cuba's inflation rate, trade deficit, and external debt also provide useful insights into the state of its economy. Because all prices are fixed, there is no official inflation rate in Cuba. Indeed, since 1967, the government has provided all economic data in current prices. Nevertheless, inflation does exist and it can be calculated using the difference between the amount of money in circulation and the value of goods available to spend it on. At times there has been nearly twice as much money available as goods to buy. Thus, if prices were not fixed, they would increase 100 percent. (On average this unofficial inflation rate hovered around 80 percent annually.) Price fixing has other deleterious consequences in that it reduces the incentive to work because earning more money becomes somewhat meaningless if there is nothing on which to spend it.

Both trade deficits and external debts have increased dramatically under Castro. During the half-century before Castro, Cuba had a trade deficit only twice. In the quarter century since Castro, only twice has Cuba not had a deficit. Despite Soviet aid, Cuba has accumulated a $3.5 billion short-term debt to Western institutions. And although nearly half of the $3 to $4 billion Cuba receives annually from the Soviet Union is in the form of free equipment and subsidies, the remainder is in loans. As a result, Cuba owes over $7 billion to the Soviets, which is scheduled for repayment beginning in 1986. All told, Cuba's debt to the West is nearly 60 times what it was before Castro. It is over 200 times greater if the Soviet debt is included.

Measuring Growth

Cuba's economic performance since 1959 can also be evaluated using standard macro-economic indicators (e.g., national income accounts, savings rate, investment rate) to measure economic growth. Here again, Cuban data presents several problems. Cuba's national accounts do not follow the Western concept of gross national product

(GNP) but rather use Soviet techniques of gross social product (GSP) and gross material product (GMP). Furthermore, Cuba's techniques for measuring GSP and GMP have varied at times over the last 25 years. And as we have already discussed, there is significant uncertainty about the impact of inflation on economic data over time. Nevertheless, there are various estimates of Cuban economic growth available.

Using official Cuban sources for GSP and GMP, for example, the following growth rates are produced. (Note: the 1976-1980 growth rates are estimated not actual.) (See Table 1)

From the above chart several overall conclusions may be drawn about Cuba's economic growth. First, economic growth has been quite uneven over the revolutionary period, and Communist Cuba has plainly been unable to generate sustained high-rates of economic growth. Although overall economic growth occurs in the period 1960 to 1980, most of the expansion occurred between 1973 and 1980. Between 1960 and 1973 the economy was virtually stagnant and, in fact, declined steadily in per capita terms.

Second, the periods of relative economic prosperity remained closely linked with world sugar prices, thus providing further evidence of Cuba's economic vulnerability, a vulnerability caused in part by its lack of economic diversification. The expansion that took place after 1973 was mainly the result of skyrocketing world sugar prices. In addition, because of highly subsidized Soviet oil, which provides over 97 percent of Cuba's total oil consumption needs, Cuba emerged unscathed from the mid-1970's oil price rise. Thus, increased sugar revenues allowed for a temporary rise in investments that yielded returns even after sugar prices plummeted in 1976. Third, changes in output since the early 1960s were mixed. In absolute terms, the agricultural sector in the mid-1970s was barely above 1959 levels. This represents, however, a 60 percent decline in per capita terms. The industrial sector recorded some gains in intermediate products (nickel and steel) but showed poor results in consumer goods.

There is another body of research, albeit incomplete, that suggests growth rates approximately one half of those determined using official Cuban sources. This research concludes that 1959 and 1960 were clearly periods of great economic expansion resulting from the reutilization of previously idle plants, which in turn led to greater production and general increases in buying power. But 1962 and 1963 were years of economic chaos as a result of widespread expropriations and mismanagement. Economic growth estimates for this period range from -8 to -20 percent. The research also suggests that

25

TABLE 1
ECONOMIC GROWTH IN CUBA, 1962–1980

YEARS	GSP (In Million Pesos)	GMP	ANNUAL RATES TOTAL (%)	ANNUAL RATES PER CAPITA (%)	STAGE AVERAGES TOTAL (%)	STAGE AVERAGES PER CAPITA (%)
1962	6,082.1	3,698.2	—	—		
1963	6,013.2	3,736.7	1.0	-1.6		
1964	6,454.5	4,076.4	9.0	6.4	5.2%	2.7%
1965	6,770.9	4,137.5	1.5	-1.0		
1966	6,709.3	3,985.5	-3.7	-5.7		
1967	7,221.6	4,081.0	2.4	0.5		
1968	7,330.9	4,352.6	6.7	5.0	0.4%	-1.3%
1969	7,236.1	4,180.6	-4.0	-5.6		
1970	8,355.6	4,203.9	0.6	-0.9		
1971	8,936.4	4,818.2	14.6	12.8		
1972	10,349.2	6,026.9	25.1	23.0		
1973	11,910.3	6,710.4	11.3	9.4	16.3%	14.5%
1974	13,423.5	7,414.1	10.5	8.9		
1975	15,799.3	8,886.3	19.8	18.3		

TABLE 1 (continued)

ECONOMIC GROWTH IN CUBA, 1962–1980

YEARS	GSP (In Million Pesos)	GMP	ANNUAL RATES[a] TOTAL (%)	ANNUAL RATES[a] PER CAPITA (%)	STAGE AVERAGES[a] TOTAL (%)	STAGE AVERAGES[a] PER CAPITA (%)
1976	15,860.5	8,881.8[c]	-0.1	-1.5		
1977	16,510.8[b]	9,246.0[c]	4.1	2.9		
1978	18,062.8[b]	10,115.2[c]	9.4	8.4	4.1%	3.1%
1979	18,830.5[b]	10,545.1[c]	4.3	3.6		
1980[d]	19,395.4	10,861.4[c]	3.0	2.3		

[a]GMP; in 1962–1966 at constant prices, in 1977–1980 in current prices.

[b]Official Cuban Estimate.

[c]Author estimate based on the average ratio of GMP/GSP in the previous ten years.

[d]Goal

SOURCES: GSP 1962–1966 *Boletín 1966*, p.20; 1967–1969 *Anuario 1972*, p.31; 1970 *Anuario 1973*, p.35; 1971–1974 *Anuario 1975*, p.39; 1975–1976, *Anuario 1976*, p.45; 1977 *La economía Cubana 1977*, p.1; 1978 *La economía cubana 1978*, p.5; *Granma Weekly Review*, 6 January 1980, pp.2–3; GMP 1962–1966 *Boletín 1966*, p.20; 1967–1975 *Banco Nacional de Cuba*, 1977, p.11; A new GSP series for 1975–1978, with a different methodology, appears in *Anuario 1978*, p.50.

(Carmelo Mesa-Lago, *The Economy of Socialist Cuba: A Two Decade Appraisal* (Albuquerque: University of New Mexico Press, 1981), p.35.)

from 1965 to 1967 the Cuban economy grew at less than 3 percent per year in real GNP. This was followed by a period of economic stagnation lasting until 1972. Thus, in real terms, the Cuban economy in 1973 was at 1965 levels, with the latter not much above 1959 levels. Of course, per capita economic levels declined steadily over this period at a rate of approximately 1.25 percent (using the general population growth rate) annually.

Beginning in 1973 through 1978 there appears to have been significant economic growth, though at far lower rates than that suggested by Cuban data. Growth rates in the period 1973 to 1978 probably averaged 4 to 5 percent annually in real GNP. Again one must subtract about 1.25 percent to arrive at approximations of per capita growth. 1979 and 1980 were lackluster years followed by a strong year in 1981 and a poor performance in 1982. In the future, Cuba's economic growth is likely to be minimal because of depressed world sugar prices and the need for Cuba to service its large foreign debt.

International Comparisons

Cuba in the 1950s was not one of the poorest countries in Latin America, it was, in fact, one of the more developed countries. Under Castro's rule, however, Cuba has become one of the lesser developed Latin American countries. (See Tables 2 and 3)

While Cuba's economy has expanded little, if at all, most other Latin American countries have developed their economies with greater success. Tables 2 and 3 indicate the extent to which Cuba's economy has changed in relation to the rest of Latin America. From 1952 to 1981, Cuba dropped from the third highest GNP per capita in Latin America to the fifteenth. In Table 4, the extent to which Cuba has failed to diversify economically under Castro is contrasted with the extent to which other Latin American countries have succeeded in diversifying their economies.

The Nature of Cuba's Economy

The nature of the Cuban economy and the reasons for its generally poor economic performance under Castro are attributable to internal as well as external causes. Cuba's failure to diversify its economic base—the perpetuation of its sugar-based monoculture—and its weak growth record are primarily the result of Castro's political objectives taking priority over economic objectives. Other related explanations include attempts to impose dogmatic Marxist-Leninist principles on

TABLE 2
RELATIVE POSITION IN LATIN AMERICA IN
GNP PER CAPITA

POSITION	1952	1981	CHANGE IN POSITION
1	Venezuela	Venezuela	—
2	Argentina	Uruguay	4
3	Cuba	Argentina	−1
4	Chile	Chile	—
5	Panama	Mexico	3
6	Uruguay	Brazil	1
7	Brazil	Panama	−2
8	Mexico	Paraguay	10
9	Colombia	Costa Rica	1
10	Costa Rica	Colombia	−1
11	Dominican Rep.	Dominican Rep.	—
12	Guatemala	Ecuador	4
13	El Salvador	Peru	4
14	Nicaragua	Guatemala	−2
15	Honduras	Cuba	−12
16	Ecuador	Nicaragua	−2
17	Peru	El Salvador	−4
18	Paraguay	Honduras	−3
19	Bolivia	Bolivia	—
20	Haiti	Haiti	—

SOURCES: Table prepared by Jorge Sanguinetty and Ernesto Betancourt on the basis of data from the *World Development Report 1983* for 1981 figures and the "Tipologia Socio-Economica de los Paises Latino-americanos" published in a special issue of *Revista Interamericana de Ciencias Sociales,* Vol. II., OAS Secretariat, Washington, D.C. 1963.

the economic system, the impact of Cuba's military policies, and the effects of the U.S. commercial embargo.

The Cuban economy lacks necessary information, qualified managers and technicians, and economic policies, across all sectors, are inconsistent. The economic system is firmly centralized and elementary in terms of management, decision making, and overall direction. As a result, there is evidence of a plantation mentality in which those at the production level, being totally dependent on decisions made at the center, are generally indifferent to economic goals and objectives. From the individual's perspective there is little incentive to increase personal productivity, hence, worker produc-

TABLE 3
GNP PER CAPITA 1981 (DOLLARS)

Venezuela	4220
Uruguay	2820
Chile	2560
Argentina	2560
Mexico	2250
Brazil	2220
Panama	1910
Paraguay	1630
Costa Rica	1430
Colombia	1380
Dominican Republic	1260
Jamaica	1180
Ecuador	1180
Peru	1170
Guatemala	1140
Cuba	*880-1110*[a]
Nicaragua	860
El Salvador	650
Honduras	600
Bolivia	600
Haiti	300

SOURCES: Table prepared by Jorge Sanguinetty and Ernesto Betancourt on the basis of data from the *World Development Report 1983* World Bank, Oxford University Press, 1983.
[a]Although in 1982 the World Bank stopped providing specific estimates for Cuban GNP per capita, it locates Cuba within the group of countries having the above range.

tivity and efficiency suffers. In addition, a type of guerrilla mentality has characterized economic planning. Goals are set and pursued with little regard for efficiency or the relationship between supply and demand.

Because Cuba's economy is centrally planned and not responsive to market mechanisms, efficiency is not its most notable characteristic. Cuban economic planning is concerned with maximum output, but unlike a market economy, production and opportunity costs are much less significant. Managers at production levels are primarily concerned with fulfilling production quotas and have little regard for economic efficiency. Thus, in past years during the sugar cane harvest it was not uncommon for nearly the entire country to inter-

TABLE 4

PERCENTAGE SHARE OF MERCHANDISE EXPORTS

	PRIMARY COMMODITIES		MANUFACTURES	
	1960	1980	1960	1980
Cuba	95	95	5	5
Costa Rica	95	66	5	34
Dominican Republic	98	76	2	24
El Salvador	94	61	6	39
Guatemala	97	76	3	24
Haiti	100	—	0	—
Honduras	98	88	2	12
Jamaica	95	47	5	53
Nicaragua	98	86	2	14
Panama	—	81	—	9
Argentina	96	77	4	23
Bolivia	—	97	—	3
Brazil	97	61	3	39
Chile	96	80	4	20
Colombia	98	80	2	20
Ecuador*	99	97	1	3
Mexico	88	61	12	39
Paraguay	100	88	0	12
Peru	99	84	1	16
Uruguay	71	62	29	38
Venezuela*	100	98	0	2

SOURCE: Table prepared by Jorge Sanguinetty and Ernesto Betancourt on the basis of data from the *World Development Report 1983,* World Bank, Oxford University Press, 1983.
*primary commodity = petroleum

rupt normal activity to participate in the harvest. The opportunity costs for such practices, albeit difficult to measure, are sizable.

Cuba continues to engage in much economic activity that is inefficient. For example, Cuba is committed to the nickel industry for political reasons and because it is a significant foreign exchange earner. Although the nickel industry is energy intensive, Cuba is able to purchase this energy from the Soviet Union at highly subsidized prices, thus enabling Cuba to earn much needed foreign currency through exports of nickel that would be inefficient to produce and sell without Soviet largesse.

In contrast, Cuba's most impressive achievement has been the expansion of the fishing industry, particularly the overseas operations. Cuba's deep sea fishing industry started from a low base of operations, but it has utilized efficient Euopean and Japanese crafts and equipment. Consequently, initial growth rates were great. In recent years, however, the industry's expansion has slowed because of growing restrictions by many countries on foreign fishing in their territorial waters.

Economics and Ideology

Cuba's poor economic performance is partly attributable to ideological radicalism. The extreme and dogmatic application of Marxist-Leninist teachings and Fidelista tenets to economic problem solving has proved a clear failure. In the 1960s and early 1970s, ideological radicalism took the form of highly-centralized economic planning and management that has led to a crippling bureaucracy and a lack of effective control over economic processes. It has forced the nationalization of virtually all means of production; at present over 95 percent of the economy is state run. Occasional attempts to allow small pockets of privately owned enterprises to operate, particularly in agriculture, have been short-lived despite, or perhaps because of, the significantly higher productivity of these businesses. An overreliance on moral incentives—noneconomic rewards for work— has clearly contributed to the worker's low productivity and high absenteeism. The emphasis on revolutionary loyalty over technical expertise as a hiring criteria is largely responsible for the flight of managers and technicians in the early 1960s and has long undermined the technical preparation of the regime's own cadres.

The impact of ideology, however, has varied over the years. When, for example, sugar prices rose in the 1970s and some growth occurred, ideological constraints were temporarily eased. After courting economic disaster in the late 1960s by implementing the utopian economic policies advocated by Ernesto "Che" Guevara, the Cuban leadership publicly acknowledged its "idealistic" mistakes and, after 1970, embarked on a process of "rectification." The most recent trends indicate, however, an austere economic future and a reemphasis on so-called moral incentives.

Political Priorities

Beyond strict ideological considerations, the Cuban economy is fundamentally dependent on a number of exogenous factors. The primary one remains Fidel Castro's ability to give the highest priority to political decisions and to subject the economic process to fulfilling his political objectives. The economy is subservient to Castro's personal power, and Castro remains surprisingly involved in the operation of individual enterprises. The excessive centralization that has characterized the Cuban economy is partly a result of Castro's desire to centralize political power. Any attempt to make the economy more productive and efficient would involve a relaxation of centralized controls, greater decision-making power at the local levels, and consequently, a redistribution of political power. Local managers would need to be able to make independent decisions, including, for example, the hiring and firing of workers. This would be politically unacceptable to the central authorities since it would increase the managers' independence and autonomy.

The U.S. Embargo

Two additional factors with probable effects on Cuba's economic performance have been the U.S. embargo on trade with Cuba and Cuba's military establishment. With reference to the embargo, there are, in fact, two embargoes: one on trade and one on finance and investments. Initially, the trade embargo had a definite negative impact on Cuba, particularly as it caused shortages and disruptions in supplies. Over time, however, this impact has diminished as new suppliers have been found to replace the United States. The effect of the embargo on Cuban sugar production was also short-lived as substitute markets were quickly found. In all likelihood, more damage was probably done to the Cuban sugar industry by the expansion and protection of the European sugar beet industry than by the U.S. boycott.

On the other hand, the impact of the embargo on finance and investments has grown over the years. Although Cuba recently has tried to attract foreign investment, so far their efforts have been unsuccessful. From a foreign investor's perspective, there is no economic motivation to locate a plant in a country where no market is available for the goods. In addition, the uncertainties concerning Cuban behavior toward foreign investors creates an uncomfortable psychological environment.

In contrast to the preceding debate, there are some who argue that the overall impact of the U.S. economic embargo has been marginal and, to a certain extent, even beneficial for Cuba. As this argument goes, the net effect of the embargo has been to prevent Cuba from engaging in economic activity for which it would be unqualified—investment expenditures. In the absence of the U.S.

boycott one could assume that investment expenditures would have been much higher, the lack of managerial efficiency would have been little affected, and Cuba would have committed itself to sizable loans without an enhanced ability to repay because of inefficient management. Clearly, these conclusions are debatable. Nonetheless, though the impact of the embargo may not be as extensive as the United States had hoped it would be, the issue at stake is political, not economic: as long as Castro uses foreign currency earnings to support activities that are detrimental to U.S. interests, an embargo should remain in place.

Military

Although it is difficult to arrive at any definite conclusions about the economic impact of Cuba's military establishment, it is possible to draw some broad generalizations. The greatest difficulty, of course, is the lack of data on pricing and costs involved in Cuban military expenditures. Nonetheless, it is sufficient to note that Cuba has the second largest military establishment in Latin America; its military is 10 times larger in per capita terms than that of Brazil. Moreover, in addition to the absolute costs involved in maintaining such large armed forces, there are enormous opportunity costs incurred as a result of the military absorbing the best talent in the country for generally nonproductive purposes. On the other hand, the intangible benefits that Cuba generates from its security relationship with the USSR are significant economically, if difficult to quantify. The extensive security establishment generates Eastern bloc financial subsidies. In the case of Cuba's adventures in Africa, it also sometimes generates sizable foreign currency earnings. Angola reportedly pays $250 million annually for Cuba's military presence. This security relationship, however, sustains an artificial sense of economic activity. Also, these activities represent a long-term time bomb; in the event that a rapid repatriation of troops is required, Cuba would likely face exacerbated employment problems.

Concluding Comments

Analysts of Cuba's economy disagree over whether substantial changes have occurred in the basic features of the economy, and if so, to what extent. There are some who argue that Cuba's economy has changed substantially since the 1960s. The argument follows that there has been some movement, albeit small, away from the previous inertia, disorganization, excessive centralization, and over-reliance on moral incentives. Though it is unlikely to reach very far, there has been over time a shift toward some decentralization, increased use of material incentives, and more realistic and sophisticated planning.

There are others who argue that any semblance of decentralization is superficial and misleading. Despite the introduction of the first five year plan in 1976 and attempts to implement some systemic innovations, significant changes simply have not occurred. The system still functions in a way that provides neither the initiative nor the means for managers to increase productivity or efficiency. There is no evidence of streamlining or sophisticated management. Indeed, most production decisions still originate at the top with little regard for actual production capabilities. Under these circumstances any substantial economic changes would inevitably require, and result in, some measure of political decentralization; an event unlikely to occur easily under Castro. Under present and foreseeable conditions the Soviet Union is not apt to allow Cuba's economy to deteriorate to the point where it would either collapse or create sufficient pressures for political change. Thus, significant economic change does not appear imminent.

The shape of the Cuban economy is unlikely to change in any major form while Fidel Castro remains in power. Nevertheless it would be foolish to discount any change as impossible. It is important to remember that a new generation of Cubans has emerged since 1959. A younger generation of managers, bureaucrats, and technocrats are reaching high levels of authority. This new generation differs in many ways from the small guerrilla elite that has ruled for over 25 years. As technocrats, their priorities are likely to be somewhat different from those who participated in the revolution. With greater technical training and less of a guerrilla and siege mentality, it is conceivable that they might place a lower value on political priorities and a greater one on economic development. What this portends for Cuba's future economic performance is not yet clear and in any event is some time away. For now it is sufficient to note that although the Cuban economy has survived—admittedly, against great odds—it could not have done so without large-scale Soviet aid, and this assistance seems likely to continue.

4

Cultural Dimensions

Introduction

The very nature of a totalitarian regime, in which all aspects of a society are controlled by the state, makes it difficult to examine the evolution of one isolated dimension of society. Any study of the impact of the Castro regime on Cuban culture must therefore first outline the pre-revolutionary cultural tradition. Cuban culture in the 1980s has arrived at a point that emphasizes unquestioned obedience to the ebb and flow of the government's fervor.

The early years of the revolution generated considerable vigor and intellectual enthusiasm. But that process of artistic expression collided with the fledgling notions of the role of culture in a Communist society. Thus by 1961, the cultural ideals associated with liberal democracy were pushed aside by Fidel Castro's open identification with Marxism-Leninism. In the process, influential vehicles of political doctrine such as the newspaper *Revolución,* and its editor Carlos Franqui, were pressured into dogmatic conformity. And by the end of the 1960s, following a brief period of relative Cuban ideological autonomy vis-a-vis the Soviet Union, the Castro regime's ideology returned to the conventional Soviet mold—reinforcing trends generated in the early years of the revolution. By the end of the 1960s, Cuba's version of Marxism-Leninism was no more than a regurgitation of the official Soviet theological interpretation.

The 1970s opened with what some have characterized as the Stalinization of Cuban culture, primarily in literature and art. Intellectual diversity was reduced to the point where personal attitudes were forced to emulate rigid governmental guidelines. Nonconformity was confronted with immediate ostracism from the state-recognized artistic circles; an action that cut all links between the artist and the world of art. In addition, the regime often resorted to torture, incarceration, or exile for recalcitrant artists. Cuba's deplorable record in the cultural arena clearly cuts across related experiences in the legal and human rights domain.

Cuban Cultural Tradition

During the nineteenth century, Cuban culture revolved around two mutually reinforcing ideas: the creation of a national conscience and opposition to the Spanish colonial regime. After the wars for independence, the century ended with the generation of Cuba's foremost thinker and writer, José Martí, who died in 1895 while fighting against Spain. The accomplishments of Martí and other writers, poets, and essayists were so impressive that in the twentieth century Mexican historian Carlos Pereyra wrote, "no Latin American nation began its independence with such a brilliant cultural tradition as Cuba." The price of independence, though, was high, and a feeling of frustration and disillusionment spread among an intellectual elite decimated by war.

During the first two decades of the republic, efforts to revitalize the idea of nationalism took place in an atmosphere of pessimism. In 1923, following a period of economic crisis, young intellectuals protesting against political corruption heralded a new national attitude.

The struggle against Machado's dictatorship (1928-1933) forced this new generation to sacrifice many cultural projects in order to take a political stand. The end of this revolutionary episode brought forth nationalistic and progressive social ideas—which eventually culminated in the Constitution of 1940—and opened the way for an expanding and active native bourgeoisie. But for many intellectuals, Batista's first rise to power (1933-1939), American diplomatic intervention, as well as increasing political corruption represented a setback for their ideals.

Occasionally patronized by a new and richer upper class, cultural activities increased. Literary prizes were created, two new universities were founded in the provinces, theaters multiplied, and a group of painters and novelists gained continental reputations. Even in music, a new vitality pulsated in the work of both classical and popular composers.

Batista's military coup and second period of rule (1952-1958) did little to alter this cultural revival. During this period, Cuban intellectuals had little to do with politics, and Batista had no intention of controlling the flow of ideas in the country. Also, as the majority of Cuban artists and intellectuals intensely disliked Batista, who represented the worst of Cuba's past, few participated actively in the political struggle. What they wanted most was a quick return to political normality, to a democratic situation open to the development of all the creative forces that had been growing in Cuba since the 1920s.

Consequently, the revolutionary triumph of 1959 mobilized enthusiasm. The explosion of popular support for Castro broke their intellectual isolation and put them in contact with the masses. A new era seemed to have begun in Cuba; one in which intellectuals and artists could work with the people for a common national cause. In January 1959, in the middle of a democratic euphoria, no one envisioned the advent of a totalitarian, socialist regime.

The Impact on Culture

The crushing of Cuba's democratic institutions had a tremendous impact on the island's cultural life. The initial moments after Castro's revolutionary triumph were charged with enthusiasm; artists and intellectuals thought they could reinforce and expand Cuba's cultural tradition, and three generations coincided in this common effort. With few exceptions, the generation of 1923-1933, epitomized by Jorge Manach, placed itself at the service of a regime it considered the continuation of the frustrated revolution of 1933. The second generation, that of Fidel Castro, represented both by Catholics such as Angel del Cerro and Andrés Valdespino and independent writers such as Guillermo Cabrera Infante and Virgilio Piñera, actively cooperated in the Institute of Culture, the new National Museum, educational planning, or the exaltation of government projects. The youngest generation, Reinaldo Arenas, Herberto Padilla, Réne Leal, and many others, added their total commitment to the revolution. Carlos Franqui, editor of the semi-official newspaper, *Revolución*, issued a weekly supplement, *Lunes de Revolución*, which quickly became the forum of some of the youngest and more strident supporters of the regime. In the first issue they placed themselves at the left of the Communist party.

From January to November 1959, the majority of Cuban intellectuals and artists became increasingly apprehensive. The revolution "as Cuban as the palm trees" was becoming an anti-American, anti-democratic revolution guided by a supposedly infallible leader. Castro's growing authoritarianism, the elimination of independent magazines and newspapers, and growing pressure to support whatever the leader endorsed threatened cultural freedom. Painters and sculptors resented the official exaltation of "social realism" as the only true form of artistic expression. Dissent became dangerous, any form of criticism a counterrevolutionary act. By the end of the year, a few intellectuals had already moved into exile.

The second period (January 1960 to April 1961) witnessed the transformation of the anti-American revolution into a socialist rev-

olution and accelerated the exodus. The rise of Communist influence forced Catholics and democratic intellectuals to abandon Cuba.
The growing consensus was now in the desire to leave. Independent
journals halted publication "for lack of paper;" many of the young,
fiery writers escaped or retreated into silence. Seventy percent of
Havana's university professors, including the entire Directorate of
the Cuban Society of Philosophy, left everything behind to escape
the regime's repression.

Some of the dissidents were treated somewhat differently. García
Bercena became ambassador to Brazil and Guillermo Cabera Infante
was posted to Belgium. Eventually García Barcena refused to go
back to Cuba and died in exile. Cabrera Infante broke with the
regime in 1965. Those who remained tried to preserve a measure of
freedom inside the new socialist state. In a sort of oblique defense
of their position, they condemned Stalinism and defended the Maoist
"one hundred flowers" position. They waited for the supreme leader
to define their socialist freedom.

In June 1961, Castro addressed a National Library audience. Barely
disguising his contempt for intellectuals—even Marxist intellectuals whom he called "dogmatic bachelors of Marxism"—he gave
them his answer. He began by saying that he had been very patient
in listening to their long discussions, and that he admired their
"erudition," (in Cuba "erudito" is usually used pejoratively, like
"bookworm" is used in the United States) but Castro could not
understand their fears. Actually, there was no dilemma, no threat to
intellectual creativity. The problem was not one of freedom but of
service. Then he set the limits of their freedom: "Within the revolution, everything; against the revolution nothing!" There was no
alternative in the new Communist society.

What followed was a tragic pattern similar to that set in the Soviet
Union and other Marxist states. Some intellectuals submitted gladly
and received benefits. Others retreated to their private gardens
refusing to produce what the regime instructed. Some of the most
renowned were saved by their international reputations. The majority continued the struggle in silence. According to Roberto Valero,
Cuban poets were forced to gather in secrecy and read their poems
"as drug smugglers."

In 1968, the plight of Cuban intellectuals attracted world attention
with an incident known as the Padilla affair. That year, poet Herberto Padilla and dramatist Antón Arrufat won official literary prizes.
Both were later accused of being counterrevolutionaries. Padilla
was sent to prison and tortured. In 1971 he publically recanted his
"bourgeois" sins. Many European and Latin American intellectuals

friendly toward the Cuban revolution, including Jean Paul Sartre and Mario Vargas Llosa, expressed their concern and appealed to Castro to avoid a Stalinist taint. Castro responded by inviting all his "erudite" critics to work in the sugar fields among the Cuban peasants. "Only then intellectuals have the right to criticize what the revolution is doing." On April of that same year the first National Congress of Culture and Education issued a formal definition of the regime's artistic guidelines. "Art is a revolutionary weapon. . . . Only in the entrails of the masses can genius be found. . . . We condemn these false writers who live or have taken refuge in the decadent and rotten societies of Europe and the United States . . . they will only find the contempt reserved to traitors. . . ."

Until 1980, the official line of propaganda of the Cuban government maintained that those intellectuals who had abandoned Cuba were depraved bourgeois or "Batistianos." The names of Carlos Franqui—today living in Italy—and Guillermo Cabrera Infante, to mention only two, are enough to expose the weakness of that thesis. The Mariel exodus ratified its falsehood. Many of those who left during and after the Mariel episode were too young to have participated in or even known pre-Castro Cuba. Some of them, like Padilla, Arrufat, and Arenas, had been at times hailed by the socialist regime as brilliant children of the revolution. They brought with them from Cuba true stories of the treatment of intellectuals in Cuba. Armando Valladares, finally released after 20 years in prison for writing "counterrevolutionary" poetry, added his tragic testimony to the argument. In Cuba, Valladares declared while in Paris, " only total submission to the regime is tolerated."

Education in the Revolution

It can be argued though, and indeed the argument has been repeatedly used by the regime, that "culture" is something more than the creative capacity of the elite. Hence, the argument continues, the regime's success in educating the masses—one of the most publicized achievements of the revolutionary government—more than fully compensated for the defection of the elites. These assertions deserve close attention. Illiteracy in pre-Castro Cuba declined from 68 percent in 1900 to 35 percent in 1931. Despite many subsequent efforts by various politicians, including for example a rural education program under Batista in 1937-40, only slow and limited progress was made thereafter. In 1957 the illiteracy rate still stood at nearly 25 percent.

In the fall of 1960, Fidel Castro announced that the following year would be the Year of Education. Volunteer student teachers were organized into teaching brigades supervised by a regular teacher. In addition, large numbers of literate adults volunteered to assist in local literacy campaigns. A massive propaganda campaign was mounted to rally national support "for the most noble goal of the revolution." At the end of the campaign in December 1961 the government announced that illiteracy had been reduced to about 4 percent. Regardless of the validity of these figures the effort was a national and international success, raising the prestige of the government as one devoted to improving the welfare of the population.

The literacy campaign directed at adults was something of a crash program with tremendous short-term propaganda value, but, as the regime quickly recognized, youth education was of a greater long-term value. Under new directives, the number of schools and teachers multiplied. In 1958-1959 there were 17,355 teachers in Cuba. One decade later this figure had risen to 47,876. In this same period, the number of pupils in primary schools had jumped from 700 thousand to 1.4 million. This increased emphasis on education was accompanied by a significant shift in educational goals. According to the regime, the aim of education in Cuba was no longer simply to raise the level of basic knowledge and skills, but to foster the creation of a new man; a socialist man, honest, selfless, devoted to the community, and freed from greedy and corrupt bourgeois inclinations. After 1970, the official emphasis on education seems to have declined.

Although these figures are impressive they are somewhat misleading and require further analysis. First, despite claims to the contrary, higher education remains quite elitist in Cuba. For example, to enter a university or the Leninist Institute, students have to pass several screening tests that measure their level of participation in Communist youth organizations. Second, the overall purpose of education at all levels is to produce better Communists, men and women unconditionally loyal to the party and the party leadership. (Article 38 of the Cuban Socialist Constitution states that the purpose of education is to promote the formation of the communist character of the new generations.) Classroom texts and discussion are limited to Marxist topics and, as in the rest of society, dissent is tolerated only within the party framework—"within the revolution everything; against the revolution nothing." And finally, after more than 25 years of new socialist education, the achievements are far more modest than those initially proclaimed. For example, in the fall of 1980, Education Minister Jose R. Fernández declared, "we have not achieved the required level of efficiency and exigency in our administrative structure or in our educational activity." According to other official sources, more than 40 percent of science laboratories in secondary schools were out of order at any given time. Many schools were deteriorating because of faulty construction and inadequate maintenance, while others suffered from deficient lighting and ventilation. School dropout rates are rising again, and perhaps more symptomatic and distressing for the regime's image, it was found that 34 percent of all secondary schools were engaged in some form of academic fraud, or cheating, on the part of students and faculty.

Similarly, not even Marxist scholarship seems to have gained much from the revolution. The most frequently cited Cuban Marxist scholars, Julio LeRiverand and Moreno Fraginals, are members of a pre-revolutionary generation. In 1967, Jorge Ibarra published *Historia de Cuba,* a much touted example of the new wave of Marxist scholarship that would soon flourish in Cuba. This new wave recieved a serious blow two years later when a visiting Polish Marxist scholar, Tadeus Lapkowski, published in Havana a devastating critique of *Historia de Cuba.* The Pole warned his Cuban comrades against falling into the easy trap of substituting cliches and propaganda for the serious study of Cuban history.

Popular Culture

Along with the fine arts, popular culture in Cuba, that is the music, literature, art, dance, theater, and film enjoyed by the broad sections of the population, has lost its creative zeal under a regime that restricts artistic freedom and individualism. Cuba, which prior to Castro was one of the leading centers of Latin dance music, has since failed to contribute to the rich body of Latin American popular music. Indeed, Cuba's more renowned composers, musicians and vocalists went into exile in the early part of the Castro regime. And from all indications the current Cuban artistic environment has not improved. During the recent tour in the United States of a well-known and officially backed Cuban music group "Irakere," two of the group members defected because of lack of artistic freedom in Cuba. They complained, for instance, that in Cuba one can only play jazz music if it is labeled "progressive socialist music." Moreover, many major poets—Armando Valladares is one notable example—have either gone into exile or have been imprisoned. In the film industry as well, Cuba's most respected and acclaimed film makers and actors have defected to the West in search of artistic freedom.

In 1964, in a famous interview in Paris, novelist Alejo Carpentier was asked why he had not written a novel about the Cuban revolution. He answered that unfortunately he had been raised and educated long before the revolution and the burden of creating new revolutionary novels would have to fall on the shoulders of a younger generation. "Twenty years from now," he affirmed, " we will be able to read the literary products of the new Cuba." Those 20 years have elapsed. Tragically, the Cuban revolution cannot offer a single notable novelist, a famous poet, a penetrating essayist, nor even a fresh contribution to Marxist analysis. Cuba's brand of Marxism-Leninism is viewed, by the Soviets, as being obsolete. Cuban ideology is based upon the orthodox 1920's brand of Leninism, and whole schools of Marxist thought have evolved since then. Censorship and fear have smothered creativity in Cuba. What is left on the island is merely the incessant voice of official propaganda.

5

The Social Dimensions

___

Introduction

The transformation of Cuba's political and economic systems has been accompanied by profound changes in Cuban society. Extensive and arbitrary reforms have reordered Cuba's pre-1959 social structure and introduced a level of state involvement in national affairs unprecedented in pre-1959 Cuba. Thus, the impact of Castro's transformation on Cuban society has been a point of considerable debate. Data indicating general socioeconomic improvement—such as the rise in health and educational indices—are often cited as evidence that the Castro regime has plainly improved the lot of most Cubans. But figures cited alone and out of context can be misleading. Socioeconomic change is best understood not in isolation but in a comparative context. Thus a balance sheet of social change under Castro should include: comparisons with other countries, and considerations to the price paid by society.

The Balance Sheet Part I: Improvements ?

Judging Changes in Society

During the course of the revolution, numerous changes have occurred in Cuban society. Health, education, and social mobility are often cited as areas of major improvement brought about by Castro's regime. To a degree, the regime may take credit for several instances of social progress, particularly in extending basic services to a larger portion of the population. Many Cubans who had little or no access to basic health care and educational opportunities before 1959, now do. Consequently, many health and education indicators have improved. Cuba claims that its illiteracy rate is approximately 2 percent (it is probably about 6 percent), life expectancy is over 70 years, and infant mortality rates are 19 per thousand, all nearly at

44

Western levels. Moreover, enrollment rates as well as graduation rates have increased.

In many cases, however, the appearance of progress may be misleading. Many of the improvements that occurred after Castro came to power had little to do with the revolution. Rather, these improvements were a continuation of trends present before 1959 and were often due to improvements in technology or health care techniques. (see Table I)

Table I: Socioeconomic Indicators

Average life expectancy:	70 years
Infant mortality:	19 per thousand
Illiteracy rate:	3-6%
Percent of population with: completed primary education or less:	59%
completed secondary education or less:	38%
completed higher education or less:	3%

The Cuban government has claimed that it is responsible for the eradication of diseases such as measles and polio. Both diseases, in fact, have been eradicated in Cuba and elsewhere as a result of medical breakthroughs unrelated to Cuba or to Castro. Increases in the percentage of the population with completed educations can be partially accounted for by the population boom that raised Cuba's population from 6.5 million in 1959 to 10 million in 1981, thereby raising proportionally the percentage of school aged youth in the overall population.

Indeed, comparable, and sometimes superior indices are now often found in countries that 25 years ago had lower standards than Cuba and the fact that they have been accomplished without the concomitant loss of political and economic freedoms is clear testimony to the failure of the revolutionary pro-Soviet model of development. For instance, while in 1959 certain indices in Cuba were more favorable than those in Spain, Germany, Italy, and Puerto Rico, in 1980 the positions were reversed. For example, in this period the infant mortality rate dropped from 32 to 19 deaths per thousand while Spain's fell from 50 to 10 per thousand. Costa Rica, an open, pluralistic, nonmilitarized, democracy in Central America is a notable example of the fact that a society need not be politically repressive to be socioeconomically progressive. Low unemployment, relatively high standards of living, high health standards, and low illiteracy rates do not require the abolition of individual rights and political pluralism nor the imposition of dogmaticism, censorship or militarism. Indeed, Costa Rica enjoys socioeconomic standards roughly equivalent to Cuba in nearly all categories. Yet Costa Ricans also enjoy freedom of expression without political repression, freedom of mobility, and freedom from the requirement to shed blood in distant continents for the simple purpose of advancing an entrenched dictatorship's political ambitions.

Housing

In housing, the revolution made an initial positive impact, but new housing construction was soon neglected. The result has been a housing crisis that is yet to be resolved. The unavailability of new housing has created problems ranging from the growing numbers of shanty towns to the increased stress on the family. The latter is particularly prevalent among newly married couples who must often live with their families in already crowded conditions.

Social Mobility

In the immediate aftermath of the revolution in 1959, there was a radical transformation in the pattern of social mobility. There were widespread promotions and opportunities for people previously outside the range of normal political, social, and economic activity. As the revolutionary regime consolidated itself, however, and as the social hierarchy became increasingly stratified and closed, social mobility patterns became stagnant. For the most part, the opportunities for mobility that were available in the early 1960s are no longer present.

As a result, the normally troublesome generation gap has been exacerbated. Nearly 50 percent of the Cuban population was born after 1959 and they have only the Castro regime for their frame of reference. This generation did not experience the anti-Batista struggle and may be less likely to accept that after more than 25 years of constant sacrifices and unfulfilled promises, more sacrifices will be necessary to achieve political participation. Moreover, this generation of generally better educated youth is more apt to be discontented with a repressive system led by the same small circle of leaders who are less able to fulfill their rising expectations and growing ambitions. For them Cuba is socially and politically ossified and economically stagnant.

Women

Theoretically, Cuban men and women have equal rights and freedoms. In practice the record is mixed. Although some progress has been made in improving the status of women, there is evidence that women continue to play their traditional social roles. Significant change has been hindered by both cultural resistance and adverse economic conditions. Efforts to increase employment for women have not met expectations, despite the occasional large-scale use of voluntary female labor. Between 1953 and 1970, labor force participation among women aged 15 and over increased from 13.7 to 16.0 percent. By 1979, the rate of female labor force participation reached only 31 percent, a level attained or surpassed in other Latin American countries. Moreover, women continue to be over-represented in the service sector of the economy and under-represented in leadership positions, particularly in senior level management.

Though few Cubans would claim that men and women in Cuba are, in fact, equal, the regime has made some efforts to improve the status of women. It must be noted again, however, that, as in other cases, the regime has exaggerated the benefits it has bestowed on women. Equal and sometimes greater accomplishments in the status of women have been achieved elsewhere without a similar price being paid.

By most accounts the social record of the Castro regime is a mixed one at best. A drastic socioeconomic transformation has taken place that has benefitted significant portions of the population to some extent, particularly those who were at the lowest end of the spectrum in pre-1959 Cuba. In effect, the regime narrowed Cuba's socioeconomic gap by officially eliminating the most privileged sector of the population and raising up the most underpriveleged. As a result, the worst examples of poverty were eliminated. Yet, the nation's aggregate wealth declined and has still to recover. Consequently in Latin American or Third World terms—a limited segment of society was relieved of abject poverty, while the rest of society, the middle class as well as what was left of the upper class, became poorer. In effect, the Castro regime redistributed poverty and rationing, not wealth; and this occurred at a substantial cost.

The Balance Sheet Part II: Costs

State Rights Versus Individual Rights

In Cuba, the relationship between the individual and the state that existed prior to 1959 has been thoroughly altered. In the name of Marxism-Leninism, the rights and interests of the individual became subservient to the rights and interests of the state. Laws and procedures were changed and organizations created to encourage and enforce the individual's conformity, discourage individualism, and punish dissent. In most Communist countries the interests of the state are determined by the party; in Cuba, however, they are determined by Fidel Castro.

The Cuban judiciary is subordinate to the executive and its role is not to interpret the law, but rather to approve it. The highest court, the "Council of Government of the People's Supreme Court," has as its primary task the transmission of the law from the executive to the lower courts. In effect, the Council of Ministers headed by Castro makes, interprets, and enforces the law.

Mass Control Mechanisms

In addition to the formal political structure modeled on Soviet institutions, Soviet influence in Cuba is evidenced in many mechanisms of direct and indirect control and repression. The Cubans, however, have made several refinements regarding the Soviet style of societal control. The most profound modification is the fundamental degree to which Cuban society is militarized.

The techniques for controlling Cuban society are complex and sophisticated, ranging from the arbitrary use of violence and terror to more subtle forms of indirect coercion. Social control mechanisms are used to impress upon society—at the mass as well as the individual level—the thorough reach and power of the regime. As a result, open dissent and opposition is often preempted before it is able to coalesce. Moreover, by judging personal political indifference or apathy as dissention, the regime effectively discourages and diffuses most passive resistance.

Political Police

Prominent among organizations devoted to vigilance and control is State Security, which is organized within the Ministry of the Interior and thus outside the military's jurisdiction. A political police force with broad and far-reaching authority and influence, State

Security's powerful position stems primarily from its special relationship with Castro. State Security, the equivalent of the Soviet KGB, can arrest and detain individuals with or without charges or trial, or even for suspicion of "potential future illegal political activities." Although State Security polices individuals suspected of real or potential illegal political activities, another state organ known as the Committees for the Defense of the Revolution (CDR) functions as a daily control mechanism for the majority of the population.

Committees for the Defense of the Revolution

With over 5 million members, the CDRs are state controlled neighborhood watch groups organized on the block level throughout Cuba. Among other functions, they watch for signs of political dissent, illegal economic activities, and other illegal behavior. The CDRs also serve to organize events such as "voluntary" field work outings and neighborhood political discussions as well as assisting in the mobilization of the population for mass rallies. As mass control mechanisms the CDRs perform both a supervisory role—as ubiquitous evidence of the regime's presence—and a regulatory role. Certificates are issued for participation in CDR activities and although the certificates themselves have limited positive application, they are used by the regime as a means to discourage political passivity. Failure to participate in CDR activities, and thus failure to collect CDR certificates, invariably results in official discrimination in matters ranging from job applications to housing permits and school applications. Continued active or even passive political dissidence usually results in imprisonment.

Political Prisoners

Though undoubtedly large, the precise number of political prisoners in Cuba remains unknown because the regime officially denies the existence of political prisoners. Nevertheless, according to Cuban officials, during the 1970s approximately 3,000 prisoners were classified as "counterrevolutionaries." Virtually all outside sources, however, including various human rights organizations cite substantially higher figures ranging from 4,000 to over 40 thousand. The precise number is unnecessary to realize the magnitude of the regime's intolerance of dissent. In Cuba, the percentage of the population imprisoned for political purposes—using government figures—is .03 percent (3,000 political prisoners in a population of 10 million). Yet, the plight of political prisoners in Cuba receives far less international attention than, say, political prisoners in the Soviet Union who represent .0004 percent of the total population. This lack of attention toward Cuban political prisoners is in addition to the fact that Cuban prisoners are treated harshly and are denied access to international organizations such as the International Red Cross or Amnesty International.

Mass control mechanisms used by the regime extend beyond such direct measures as the State Security apparatus and the CDR and include a vast array of general restrictions. Personal mobility is limited by internal passports similar to those used in the Soviet Union, and in addition to general information the passports contain personal and political evaluations. Moreoever, state permission is required to leave one's residence for over 90 days. In addition to a three year conscription period, all members of the military reserve must carry military identification papers and must report to military committees biannually to verify their health, residency, and work status. Further means of mass control include state control over all means of mass communication including television, radio, and the press. The state also preempts the possible formation of rival interest groups by permitting only the existence of state controlled mass organizations such as labor unions and youth groups.

Labor

Following a period of neglect in the 1960s, during the 1970s Cuban state controlled labor union activity was revived and reorganized. The old union structure was replaced by one that subordinates individual unions to their specific ministries. This reorganization allows unions to translate production plans into actual production more readily because the state is able to transmit its plans and targets directly to the worker and oversee the execution of these plans. The stated purpose of the unions is not to support and defend worker's rights but to support and defend the government and to improve the nation's economic performance by improving labor productivity and efficiency. The rationale behind this essentially one way arrangement is that in a "workers' state" it is unnecessary and even contradictory for unions to advocate and defend workers' rights against the state. This logical consistency, however, runs contrary to daily reality. Although Cuba may claim to be a workers' state, in the 1970s the state systematically went about increasing its control over labor. To receive employment, workers are required to have special identification cards and updated files that detail a job history and a record of labor merits and demerits as well. In addition, anti-loafing laws were passed making absenteeism—apparently a significant labor problem—punishable by arrest and imprisonment in forced labor camps.

Youth

Cuba has been beset by a perennial generation problem. In the first full generation to have matured under Fidel Castro's rule, the youth problem has manifested itself in a number of social and educational difficulties. Despite the significant advances in education made by the revolution, Cuba suffers from two serious educational deficiencies: a high dropout rate and a scarcity of technically trained graduates. Dramatic increases in school enrollments are meaningless if those who begin education fail to finish. In Cuba the dropout rate is exceedingly high. During the 1970s, over 70 percent of elementary school age children and 85 percent of high school age children dropped out. In addition, Cuba has been unable to direct sufficient numbers of students into the most needed areas. Though it produces a large number of foreign language specialists, Cuba is unable to graduate sufficient numbers of needed technicians. There is also evidence suggesting that juvenile delinquency, often directed against the state, has long been a problem in revolutionary Cuba.

Cuba has made various efforts to bring its youth related problems under control and to increase the state's influence in the life of its young people. In the last decade alone, the Young Communist League (UJC) has expanded its membership to over one million youths and has concentrated greater attention on raising its members' political consciousness, particularly by emphasizing greater indoctrination for the younger age groups. The emphasis is on instilling both revolutionary loyalty and the ethics of a selfless worker. For those immune to the UJC's persuasive techniques, there is the so-called Youth Army of Work (EJT), a paramilitary body under the armed force's jurisdiction. The EJT is a combination of former military youth organizations such as the "Compulsory Military Service," the "Youth Centennial Column," and the "Military Units to Aid Production," all of which provided military training for out of school youths and then used them as surplus labor. Approximately one-third of Cuba's youth are recruited by the EJT.

Basis of the Regime's Survival

Although it would be unrealistic to assume that the Castro regime enjoys no popular support, it is impossible to judge with certainty exactly where and how strong the support base is. In all likelihood, the Cuban public's perceptions of the regime can be classified into

51

three distinct groups: those who strongly support the regime (usually the ones who have benefitted from the revolution in terms of influence or economic position); those who fervently oppose the regime (often found in prison or exiled); and those in the middle. It is likely that the first two groups are small. The middle group, however, is probably made up of the majority of the population. They neither strongly support nor actively oppose the regime but are, instead, somewhat resigned to it. Evidence would seem to indicate that most of those in this middle group seek simply to survive, but given the opportunity, would take great risks to leave Cuba. The nature of Cuban society is such, however, that political passivity is interpreted as opposition. Consequently, the large mass in the middle is manipulated—skillfully one might add—in such a way as to make them appear to support the regime.

Despite state manipulation and pressure to conform, a large percentage of Cubans have chosen to break with the regime by emigrating. One million Cubans have left since 1959, representing some 10 percent of the total population. During a brief period in 1980, known as the Mariel incident, when Castro eased up emigration controls, 125 thousand left the country. Ironic and perhaps telling, is the fact that blue collar workers, traditionally identified by Castro as among the principal beneficiaries of Cuba's transformation, were the largest occupational group represented in this exodus.

6

Epilogue

Cuba has now been a Communist state for some 25 years. The iron certainties imposed between 1959 and 1962 with such speed and such skill have remained. The gates that ensure the commercial, intellectual, and political alienation from the United States are equally placed, despite a little fiddling with the locks in the mid-1970s. After a few years (1959-1963) of colossal agitation, civil conflict, near-war, and indeed near international war, the Cuban revolution settled into a hard stability—so stable indeed that anyone who still labels the regime a "revolution" is making one of those idiotic misuses of words in which the twentieth century is so rich. As in other Communist states, most of the leaders have remained in place for many years: Fidel Castro, the "maximum leader," "president," "commander-in-chief of the armed forces," etc.; his brother Raúl, minister of defense since 1959; Ramiro Valdés; Carlos Rafael Rodriguez; Sergio del Valle; and Osmani Cienfuegos. Their equanimity only mildly disturbed, it would seem, by the suicides of such old allies as ex-president Oswaldo Dorticós, Haydée Santamaría, or the deaths of old friends such as Che Guevara.

In some respects, Cuba is now a characteristic Communist state. As in all totalitarian systems, there has been that *Gleichschaltung* of institutions, parties, political forces, and movements that has marked the establishment of both communism and fascism. As in all Communist societies, the party controls the state. There is a stifling intellectual atmosphere: the creative writers and artists are either dead, silent, or abroad. (And that now goes for all the promising young men associated with the immensely attractive, if short-lived, "Fidelista" stage of the Cuban Revolution.) As in other Communist societies the government has managed to preserve nationalism for internal purposes and has drawn the state institutionally into an external system of alliances. The life of the spirit continues to be neglected. The forms of democratic life are preserved; there are some periodic elections and there is a constitution. But in Cuba as in other such states, these hypocritical and deceiving notions constitute tributes paid by vice to virtue. Men may be called free by their masters but there is no reality in such words unless the men concerned are able to use them.

Yet in most ways Cuba's communism is different from that which has grown up in Russia since 1917 and in other countries since 1945. Cuban communism is still a part of the family of Communist systems, as Theodore Draper put it years ago. But it is an exotic member of the family. The flavor of this tropical communism is not that it is less repressive. On the contrary, the absence of overt protest and the lack of spontaneous activity suggest that the regime is now harsher than its relatives in Europe, not that it is more popular. Nevertheless, Cuban communism is different.

The first point of difference is the origin of Cuban communism. This has cast a shadow over everything that has happened. Communism was introduced into Cuba by a leader whose appeal was such that at the beginning the people would have accepted almost anything that he said. It was the kind of macho appeal that has been exercised by many Latin American *caudillos.* Public opinion was first aroused to a tremendous pitch of excitement and then satisfied by violent revolutionary initiatives—"r-r-r-revolutionary," as Manuel Azaña put it when referring to a similar phenomenon in the Spanish Civil War. Castro imposed communism on Cuba by skillful public relations: making special use of television, by excellent timing, and by well-orchestrated intimidation. That last may not seem to be new to those who know what happened in Eastern Europe between 1945 and 1948, but intimidation was made possible because of Castro's magical personality. People who were not Communists to begin with helped Castro bully his way to absolute power. The intimidation was often carried out by *fidelistas* anxious to outdo themselves in the service of the maximum leader.

Nor was Castro a Communist in the sense of having been for many years a man who had steeped himself in Marxism, and who had won his victories by dialectical arguments with party rivals (or by the artful management of coalition rivals) as was the case in the seizure of power by, say, Rakoski in Hungary, or Gottwald in Czechoslovakia. Castro was a revolutionary, determined to carry through political change and diplomatic defiance, but he was not an orthodox party man. In the late 1950s, he made innumerable statements pledging the humanity and liberalism of his Cuban revolution. In 1959-1961 it seems that he was astute enough to see that Marxism-Leninism was a political philosophy that would justify his own dictatorship, give him external as well as internal allies, and provide a version of legitimacy for the system he was keen to establish. In these respects, Castro has been more like those leaders of the Third World who have seen Marxism-Leninism as a tool of government, not a creed. Castro's personal position, as the conqueror in a successful war (however modest the conflict may have been) was not unlike that of Tito, Hoxha, or Mao; but the way in which he imposed communism—first on himself, then on his country—was his own achievement. His subsequent personal authority, in a state where individualism has no place, is the most striking aspect of Cuba. Even the Soviet Union since Stalin has been governed by an oligarchy rather than by a single man.

Castro's abiding philosophy remains more anti-American than Marxist. The fact that this is essentially a negative creed matters less than might be supposed. Naziism also wished to destroy a past in which German history and culture had been dominated by France as much as it wished to create a thousand year reich. Castro's attitude toward the United States (as opposed, it must be conceded, to his attitude toward many individual Americans) had (and perhaps still has) the same sort of pathological character as Hitler in respect to Jewry. Here also Castro could easily align himself with leaders of the Third World who, like himself, often seek a scapegoat for their people's short-term failures under socialism as under imperialism. The United States, in the old days of Eisenhower, was the latest articulation of imperialism as well as of capitalism. It is still in Castro's propaganda as in the less violently posed affirmations of his fellow members of the group of nonaligned nations, that it is imperialism that provides the chief reason for industrial or harvest failures. This "Third Worldism" is something to which Castro has given much attention. He did not invent it: the nonaligned movement and intellectuals like Franz Fanon did that. But Castro has given it a kind of institutional form. Fanon died penniless and, apparently a patient of the CIA: Castro lives, with the CIA established as his essential object of hate.

Castro's personality has affected Cuba in other ways. He seems to be chiefly responsible for the hostility toward organization, the lack of financial discipline, the erratic planning decisions, the whimsical advocacy of unlikely products, and the institutionalized anti-institutionalism that has been the prime cause of the modest economic performance.

The relative economic failure of Cuba since 1960 is another point of difference from the rest of the Communist world. Figures in centrally controlled countries are notoriously difficult to interpret because the government is able to control them. But the overwhelming evidence is that, under state management, the Cuban economy has continued or even enhanced the role of sugar as a monocrop: the drive toward agricultural diversification which marked the efforts of governments in Cuba between 1934 and 1958 (including both of Batista's) was reversed. As a percentage of Cuban exports, Cuba's sugar currently amounts to an annual average of over 80 percent these days; it had been falling toward 60 percent in the 1950s. Sugar cultivation has been nationalized and modernized, and the crop yields are often over 8 million tons of sugar—a definite advance over the pre-Castro period. But the Cubans now have a much smaller share in the world market. Cuba sells much the same share of its crop to the Soviet Union that it used to sell to the United States. The island really has become a Soviet sugar cane plantation in lieu of that of the United States.

This reemphasis on sugar (in contrast to what was hoped so passionately by so many who supported policies of reform in 1959) makes it legitimate to argue that, while Cuba has certainly experienced a political upheaval, it has not enjoyed an economic revolution at all. The emphasis on sugar was almost certainly because of Soviet insistence in the late sixties, and it makes nonsense of the arguments put forward by economists of the school of Fernando Ortíz, and even the early editions of the *Geografía* by Antonio Nuñez Jiménez seem now sadly optimistic. A Tocqueville would certainly, at an early stage, have noticed that the Cuban revolution spawned a wholly new type of revolutionary. The point must seem especially galling to those who compare Cuba with Eastern Europe where, however much the people have suffered, the governments have been able, brutally no doubt and arbitrarily without question, to alter the industrial performance of the nations concerned.

Of course, as all analysis shows, Cuba was far from being the poorest of Latin American nations in 1958-1959. Quite the contrary, it was the third wealthiest. It would be churlish not to recognize some social changes in Cuba since 1959 which must be said to be positive. Most people point out improvements in education, health, and social services generally, while recognizing that there were in old Cuba more doctors, dentists, and hospitals per person than there are now. But these benefits were concentrated in Havana and in the upper class. Now the upper class has been destroyed and the distinction between country and town much reduced. Some Cuban medical and educational achievements have been quite impressive.

Still the question must remain as to whether these things are worth the sacrifice of freedom. It is an old Fascist as well as Communist operation to say no: the liberal state, wrote José Antonio Primo de

Rivera, has meant economic servitude because it says to workers with tragic sarcasm, "you are free to work as you wish. No one can force you to accept such and such a condition of work. But as it is we who are the rich and we offer you the conditions we like—and if you do not accept them you will die of hunger in the midst of liberal liberty." Such reflections are disdainful. The overwhelming evidence is that most people, however poor, prize liberty. Democracy gives more than simply political benefits: it can and normally does light up the dark places of corruption, and injustice of all sorts; it usually coincides with a good opportunity for economic progress; it reveals the faults or even crimes of government; and of course a stable democracy allows free trade.

There are several other ways in which Cuban communism differs from that found in East Europe. The best example is still those neighborhood snooping organizations, the Committees for the Defense of the Revolution, founded to ensure that those who desired to leave the island were not disposing principles of their goods. These bodies have now been extended it seems to Cuba's own dependency, Nicargua.

But the really significant difference between Cuban communism and its cousins is the emphasis in Cuba on weapons and men under arms, as well as the intellectual concentration of guns and violence. At an early stage in the Cuban revolution in 1961, Castro announced that, instead of a vote for every citizen, he would offer them a gun. In innumerable subsequent speeches, he insisted that he had created an armed camp in his nation. Certainly the 250 thousand permanent members of the armed forces, plus a large militia, frontier guards, and a reserve of several hundreds of thousands—no one agrees with all these numbers—together with 15 thousand state security police and a "Youth Labour Army" of 100 thousand make Cuba's armed forces the most substantial force in the Caribbean after the United States, and indeed in Latin America, after Brazil whose population is 10 times larger. Cuba's military equipment of 250 combat aircraft, its new submarines, and its armored and mechanized divisions make for a formidable enterprise that cannot be compared, in size or effectiveness, to the 50 thousand ill-trained troops of Batista's old army.

Furthermore, these armed forces have been put to use. Castro has always desired with passion to play a part in world politics. The training of these armed forces has enabled him to fulfill those ambitions. Cuban troops numbering in thousands have been sent to fight on three continents. These have been regular units, not special forces or guerrillas. Cuban tanks have been in action on the Golan

57

Heights in the war between Syria and Israel; Cuban infantry has fought South Africans as well as Jonas Savimbi's anti-communist guerillas in Angola, while large numbers of Cuban men in arms have been deployed in Ethiopia, in both the Ogaden and against Eritrea. At the same time, Cuban military advisers, in the form of palace guards or members of a training staff, have been found in almost every African country. From the coup d'état at Zanzibar in early 1963 onwards, Cubans have also been engaged in political subversion. The Tri-continental conference of 1966 was dismissed by many as promoting amateur or rhetorical backing for "wars of liberation" which afforded no great danger. As it happens, however, the Tri-continental laid the foundation for the underpinning that gave the Cubans a decisive role throughout the Third World in training guerrillas and terrorists. The line between those two has never been clear: an isolated bomb designed to cause shock and damage is a terrorist action; but if there are a hundred such bombs it is work of a guerrilla movement. In the 1960s, these movements, designed to bring radical political change in the Cuban style, were not at all effective. Since the late 1970s, there has been a renewed, more effective intervention in the Caribbean: Nicaragua, Jamaica, and Grenada all became for a time Cuban outposts, to a lesser or greater degree, and it appears that Nicaragua still is. Documents captured in Grenada after the U.S. occupation in 1983 make it clear that Grenada was nearly a satellite of the Cubans before the intervention.

No doubt, indigenous movements in these areas might have gotten underway anyway. But it is doubtful if they would have gotten so far without Cuban training, assistance, logistics, and political guidance (including such actions as ensuring unification of bands of guerrillas that threatened to be in dispute with one another). It would seem, furthermore, that Cuban involvement in international terrorism has been continuous since at least the early 1970s.

Behind Cuba in all these undertakings has been, of course, the Soviet Union: the godfather of Cuba's economic system and presumably the paymaster. The USSR is the instigator and coplanner of Cuban military, terrorist, and guerrilla operations. Doubtless there have been occasions when Cuba has taken an initiative of its own. Perhaps the opportunity opening in Angola in 1975 at the collapse of the Portuguese position was realized first by Cuba (as argued so fiercely by the Nobel Laureate and friend of Castro, Gabriel García Márquez) for Cuba had worked with the MPLA for 10 years. But the general approval and planning in these matters must have been given by the Soviet Union through one or another of its myriad shadow agencies, or indeed at one or another of the major meetings

58

between Fidel Castro or Raúl Castro, at the conference table in Moscow. Indeed, in the management of the Soviet empire, Cuba (itself a protectorate in any accurate use of the term) plays a key part; they are as it were the Soviet sepoys. (J.A. Hobson, in that famous study of empire in the 19th century, from which Lenin took many of his ideas, spoke of quibbles about the definition of "empire." The use of empire in connection with the Soviet Union seems precise and accurate.) East Germany is concerned in intelligence and in communications technology in some Soviet external adventure. Bulgaria is seen to play a major part in espionage and murder. Yemen too, trains guerillas. Most of the Soviet Union's satellites have some military use: Poland is thus the essential connection between Russia herself and the East German front line facing the West. But the combination of roles makes Cuba unique.

The functions suit Castro no doubt and those who work with him. Whether they suit anyone else in Cuba (including some Cuban Communists who may be more interested in economic achievements at home) is a different matter. Until now, of course, these external activities have been usually successful so that internal criticism has been muted. (Any successful military operation makes a thousand friends.) Such setbacks as have transpired—the Congo in Guevara's day, in 1965; Jamaica, 1980; Venezuela 1963–1964; and indeed the guerrilla generally in the 1960s—have been easy enough to confuse in the public's mind. But the fall of Maurice Bishop's regime in Grenada was a different matter. It was an overt setback. A serious setback of a similar nature in Angola might lead to a reconsideration of all of Cuba's foreign policies. Yet even here, the Soviet Union would make the determining decision. Cuba is a military camp but, as Milovan Djilas has put it, Soviet communism is "a military empire." He added "it was transformed into a military empire in Stalin's time. Internally such structures usually rot . . . but to avoid internal problems they may go for expansion . . . if it is stopped, the process of rotting will go faster." *Wall Street Journal*, February 2, 1984.

Militarization thus seems to be the Cuban regime's most striking accomplishment. Stablility has, of course, benefits of its own. We can all think of nations that have suffered from swiftly changing governments (the third and fourth Republics in France, the Weimar Republic in Germany). Actually Cuba, with all her faults between 1898 and 1959, was not one of those. The presidential system, corrupt and so enfeebling though it often was, provided an often unpopular predictability.

The Cuban people, the Cuban system, and also the problem of Cuba have now endured a very long time. Cuba continues to be a major concern to U.S. administrations in the 1980s as it has been almost continuously since 1959; and, indeed, as it has been off and on since the 1820s, an island that played a decisive part in U.S. national elections in the 1850s, the 1870s, and 1890s, as well as in the 1960s and 1970s. "What shall we do about Cuba?" has been the centuries old refrain. Cuba represents the United States's Ireland. Security, logic, and economic development would have led Cuba either to maintain the closest friendship with the United States or to join the Union, and there were Cubans who thought this desirable almost to the end of the U.S. occupation in 1902. They probably included the first president of Cuba, Tomas Estrada Palma. Similarly there were southern Catholic Irishmen who believed that Ireland would prosper if it remained part of the United Kingdom. In both cases, a strong cultural nationalism prevented annexationism. In the case of Cuba, cultural nationalism alone was inadequate: a revolutionary anti-U.S. internationalism was alone strong enough. Even so, one-tenth of the population emigrated to the United States: "worms," they were called by Castro, "worms who turned traitor." Castro on the other hand, sought to persuade his followers, "we are going to make the revolution, the revolution that never came about in 1898 or 1933. This time we're going to make it come true." That sentiment would not have been echoed with any enthusiasm at all by the 10,500 Cubans who fled into the Peruvian embassy in Havana on that miraculous day in 1980 when the gates were left unguarded; by the 125 thousand or so who left unexpectedly in the ensuing month; by the vast numbers of exiles who have left home to pursue freedom abroad—an exodus symbolized in the minds of many by the brave youth who with the aim of escaping to Spain hung on to the wheel carriage of an Iberia aircraft all the way across the Atlantic; and above all, by those who still linger in prisons as "plantados" (permanent prisoners).

7

Revolution in Cuba: A Brief Chronology

The revolution of 1959 was not the first in Cuban history, nor is it likely to be the last. Cuba has undergone several important revolutions, and the victory of Fidel Castro is viewed by some historians as the logical outcome of these unfulfilled events. All of these revolutions had a common theme: the desire to assert Cuba's autonomy, which to date has never really been attained. Hence the revolution of 1959 is only a part of the historical trend against outside economic and political domination, namely, that imposed by Spain, the United States, and currently the Soviet Union. Today, more than ever, Cuba remains a dependency of a foreign power and in this respect the Castro revolution has been a complete failure.

♦ *The 10 Years War (1868–1878)* began the trend of Cuban nationalism. The use of guerrilla warfare and the attitude of the United States toward Cuba became crucial factors in this struggle as they would in later Cuban revolutions. Although independence from Spain was not achieved, a national ideology was established and Antonio Maceo, Calixto García, and Máximo Gómez surfaced as national heroes.

♦ *The Second War for Independence (1895)* was a continuation of the first unsuccessful revolution. During its early stages, José Martí, the father of Cuban independence, organized support in the United States and was tragically killed while fighting with guerrilla forces. The intervention of the United States (the Spanish-American War of 1898) broke Cuba's colonial ties to Spain, but did not result in complete independence. Defining the nature of Cuban-American relations, the Platt Amendment made Cuba a protectorate with a subtle form of American domination.

♦ *United States Interventionism (1898–1934)* compromised Cuban sovereignty but was legally justified by the Platt Amendment. These interventions ranged from landing marines on Cuban

61

soil to sending special proconsuls to exert diplomatic pressure on Havana. Objectively, however, Cuba did retain some political autonomy and more than one intervention was encouraged by Cuban politicians who were adept at manipulating the colossus of the north.

♦ *Batista and the Constitution of 1940.* From 1934 to 1944 Batista eased American concerns about stability in Cuba during a period of international turmoil. In 1944 he stepped down from power, respecting the liberal democratic Constitution of 1940 which he had allowed to be drawn up. Yet a new era of political democracy was damaged by the corruption of the subsequent Grau San Martín and Prío Socarrás regimes. In 1952 Batista himself laid the basis for the revolution of 1959 when his coup ousted the legitimate government and thus began to modify the rules of the game established by the 1940 constitution.

1952 March

General Fulgencio Batista overthrows the government of President Carlos Prío Socarrás in a military coup.

1953 July

Fidel Castro leads small band of rebels in failed attack on the Moncada Cuban army barracks in Santiago de Cuba; about 100 students and soldiers killed. Castro escapes but is soon arrested, convicted, and imprisoned. The Bishop of Santiago and other civic leaders pressured the regime to guarantee the lives of those who had been captured.Later Castro is released in a general amnesty and goes into exile in Mexico. Castro's rebel group becomes known as the 26 July Movement.

1956 April

Col. Ramón Barquín and a group of army officers are arrested for plotting a coup. They acknowledge conspiring against the regime and many. are sentenced to 8-years in prison. About 100 officers are expelled from the armed forces.

April

About 100 men attack the army base Goicuría in the city of Matanzas. Many are killed.

November

Castro leaves Mexico with 86 followers aboard a small sailing vessel, the Granma. He lands in Cuba and, although pursued by the military, manages to escape with a dozen survivers into the Sierra Maestra mountains where he establishes his rebel base.

1957 March
About 100 men stormed Batista's palace. Jose Antonio Echevarría, President of the Federation of University Students (University of Havana) was killed in a shootout with the police.

September
Mutiny at Cienfuegos Naval Base. The city of Cienfuegos fell to the rebels. Batista used bombers, tanks, and armored cars in the fight and several hundred were killed. Lt. San Román, leader of the rebels, was captured. He was tortured for months and later killed without having had a trial.

1958 March
The United States suspends all arms shipments to Batista.

April
General strike called by the 26 July Movement, and the civic resistance fails.

November
Election held. Batista claims victory for his candidates.

1959 January
Batista resigns and flees to the Dominican Republic. The 26 July Movement takes over virtual control of the government, and Castro marches into Havana.

February
Castro sworn in as premier of Cuba.

April
Castro visits the United States.

May
Agrarian Reform Bill effectively expropriates American owned sugar properties.
Cuban-organized expeditions land in the Dominican Republic, Haiti, Nicaragua, and Panama. Without local support, they all fail.

1959 October/November
Pro-Soviet factions within the revolutionary government consolidate control of the army, the bureaucracy, and the labor movement.

1960 February
Cuba and the USSR sign sugar agreement.

May
United States cuts financial aid to Cuba. Virtual censorship imposed in Cuba.

June
The United States and Great Britain reject Cuban demands that their companies in Cuba refine Soviet crude oil. U.S. cuts Cuban sugar quota by 95 percent. Havana nationalizes all remaining American properties.

July
Khrushchev threatens Soviet retaliation if U.S. intervenes militarily against Cuba.

September
Cuba receives first Soviet military aid.

1960-
61   Second wave of Cuban refugees begins. The first group, in early 1959, had been associated with the ancien regime.

1961 January
United States severs diplomatic relations with Cuba.

April
Bay of Pigs invasion.

May
Castro proclaims Cuba a socialist state in his May Day speech.

1962 January
USSR and Cuba sign trade agreement.

October
Cuba missle crisis.

1964 July
All members of the Organization of American States (OAS), with the exception of Mexico, votes unanimously to break diplomatic and economic links with Cuba.

General: Period of aggressive Cuban exportation of guerrilla revolution throughout Latin America. Cuba's strategy of creating small guerrilla "foco" groups conflicts with Soviet strategy of working through established Latin American leftist parties. Soviet-Cuban relations deteriorate sharply.

1964-
65   Castro aids guerrilla movements in the Caribbean, Venezuela, Columbia, Perú, and Guatemala.

1965 September
More than one-quarter million Cubans arrive in the United States through the Freedom Flights program, which ended in August of 1971.

1966   January
        Tricontinental conference held in Havana. Soviet-Cuban
        tensions at a high point.
1967   October
        Ernesto "Che" Guevara, Argentine-born Cuban revolu-
        tionary leader and architect of Cuban policy of exporting
        guerrilla revolution, slain while trying to create revolution
        in Bolivia. Marks the failure and end of foco tactic.

        July
        Twenty-seven Latin American delegations met in Havana
        and the Latin American Solidarity Organization was set
        up. It included representatives from all the Latin American
        countries as well as Puerto Rico and Trinidad-Tobago.
1967
        Puerto Rican "freedom fighters" set up a "Free Puerto Rico
        Embassy" in Havana.
1968   August
        Castro supports Soviet invasion of Czechoslovakia. Marks
        beginning of new phase in Cuban-Soviet relations.
1969   May
        Castro mobilizes Cuba for a sugar harvest of 10 million
        tons, the largest in Cuban history.
1970   December
        Castro acknowledges failure to meet 10 million ton sugar
        harvest target. The attempt caused the most serious eco-
        nomic and political dislocation in the history of Castro's
        rule.
        The KGB consolidates its takeover of the *Dirección Gen-
        eral de Inteligencia* (DGI), Cuba's intelligence organization.
1972   July
        Cuba admitted to the Council for Mutual Economic Assis-
        tance (COMECON), the Communist bloc trade association.
1973   October
        Cuba sends 500 tank drivers to fight for Syria in the Yom
        Kippur War with Israel.
1975   July
        OAS lifts trade embargo against Cuba.
        October
        Castro sends troops to support Soviet backed Marxist Pop-
        ular Movement for Liberation of Angola. At its peak nearly
        32 thousand Cuban troops were stationed in Angola with
        additional troops in Ethiopia, South Yemen and elsewhere.

December

First Cuban Communist Party Congress. Announcement of first Cuban Five Year Plan and ratification of new socialist constitution.

1977 March

Castro tours black Africa and visits Moscow. U.S. lifts ban on travel to Cuba.

April

Carter administration challenges Cuban presence in Zaire.

September

Tentative normalization of U.S.-Cuban relations begins with opening of interest sections. A U.S. interest section in Havana housed in the Swiss embassy and a Cuban interest section in Washington housed in the Czechoslovakian embassy.

November

United States expresses concern over the presence of 27 thousand Cuban troops in Africa.

1978 January

Cuban troops enter the war between Ethiopia and Somalia on Ethiopia's side.

1979 July

The Frente Sandinista de Liberación Nacional, with Cuban political, economic, logistical, and military assistance, overthrows the government of Anastasio Somoza in Nicaragua.

September

The Non-Aligned Movement meets in Havana and Castro is elected chairman.

1980 April

Ten thousand Cubans storm the grounds of the Peruvian embassy in Havana seeking political asylum. Taking advantage of a temporary relaxation of emigration restrictions, an additional 120 thousand Cubans aboard small boats make the exodus from the port of Mariel in Cuba to the United States.

President Carter says the presence of a Soviet Brigade in Cuba is not acceptable.

1981 January

The failure of the final guerrilla offensive in El Salvador embarrasses Cubans who backed the guerrillas and predicted a Nicaragua-like development.

February-October

As a result of the escalation of Cuban support for guerrilla movements in Latin America, Cuban relations deteriorate with Ecuador, Colombia, Costa Rica and Jamaica, all of which either break relations or withdraw their ambassadors.

February

Cuba announces a joint-venture law designed to attract foreign capital.

1982 June

Castro reports 120 thousand Cuban servicemen abroad, with an additional 30 thousand doctors, teachers, engineers and technicians, including 2,000 military advisers in Nicaragua.

November

Four high-ranking Cuban government officials indicted by a U.S. Federal grand jury on charges of smuggling narcotics into the United States.

1983 November

Cuba's presence on Grenada comes to an end; U.S. forces land on the island.

Appendix:
Project Participants

Luis E. Aguilar is professor of Latin American History at Georgetown University. Educated in Cuba, Spain, France, and the United States, his numerous publications include, *Cuba 1933: Prologue to Revolution, Marxism in Latin America* (3 editions). He is a contributor to the forthcoming *Cambridge History of Latin America*.

Juan Benemelis is a former Cuban official. Educated in Cuba he served in the Foreign Ministry and has been stationed throughout Africa.

Ernesto Betancourt is president of Trade and Development Associates, an international development consulting firm specializing in Latin America. Educated in Havana, he was, prior to 1959, the Washington, D.C. representative of the 26 July Movement and later served as managing director of the Bank of Foreign Trade, director of the National Bank, and the Cuban governor of the IMF before joining the OAS in 1960.

Cole Blasier is currently professor of Political Science at the University of Pittsburg. Dr. Blasier's publications include *Hovering Giant: U.S. Responses to Revolutionary Change in Latin America* and *The Giant's Rival: The USSR in Latin America*.

Juan Clark is professor of Sociology at Miami Dade Community College. Educated at the University of Florida, his publications include *The New Wave: A Statistical Profile of Recent Cuban Exiles to the United States*.

Sergio Díaz-Briquets is president of B-D International Consultants, a firm specializing in demographic consulting. Born in Cuba and educated at the University of Pennsylvania, Dr. Briquets has published *The Health Revolution in Cuba* and *International Migration within Latin America and the Caribbean: An Overview*.

Edward González is professor of Political Science at the University of California-Los Angeles and resident consultant at the RAND Corporation. Educated at UCLA his publications include *A Strategy for Dealing with Cuba in the 1980s* and *Cuba Under Castro: The Limits of Charisma*.

Paul Hollander was educated at Princeton and is professor of Sociology at the University of Massachusetts at Amherst and fellow at

68

the Russian Research Center at Harvard. His major publications include *Political Pilgrims-Travels of Western Intellectuals to the Soviet Union, China and Cuba.*

Irving Louis Horowitz is Hannah Arendt professor of Sociology and Political Science at Rutgers University. His most recent writings on Cuba and Latin America include *Cuban Communism* and *Beyond Empire and Revolution.*

Bruce McColm is the director for Caribbean and Central American Studies at Freedom House in New York. Educated at Harvard, Mr. McColm has written *Central America and the Caribbean: the Larger Scenario* and *El Salvador: Peaceful Revolution or Armed Struggle?*

Jorge Pérez-López is director of the Division of Foreign Economic Research at the Department of Labor. Educated at SUNY Albany, Dr. Pérez-López's publications include *Two Decades of Cuban Socialism: the Economic Context* and *Sugar and Petroleum in Cuban-Soviet Terms of Trade.*

William Ratliff is a research fellow at the Hoover Institution and a journalist. Educated at the University of Washington, Dr. Ratliff is the author of *Castroism and Communism in Latin America* and has contributed to the *Yearbook on International Communism.*

Sergio Roca is an associate professor of Economics at Adelphi University and author of *Economic Policy and Ideology in Cuba* and *Economic Policy and Institutional Change in Socialist Cuba.* Dr. Roca was educated at Rutgers University.

Jorge Sanguinetty is presently director of the Latin American Program in Applied Economics and associate professor of Economics at the American University. Born and educated in Cuba, Dr. Sanguinetty held several positions in the Cuban Finance Ministry until 1966. His publications include *Rationing and Labor Supply in Cuba* and *Methodology for Formulation of Public Sector Investment Program.*

Andrés Suarez is professor of Political Science and History at the University of Florida. Educated as a lawyer in Havana Dr. Suarez's most notable publication is his classic work *Cuba, Castro and Communism: 1959–1966.*

Lawrence Theriot is currently director of the Commerce Department's Caribbean Basin Business Information Center. Educated at George Washington University, he is the author of *Cuba Faces the Economic Realities of the 1980s.*